Handbook for Success in Whole Community Catechesis

Bill Huebsch

Handbook for
Success
in Whole
Community
Catechesis

TWENTY-THIRD PUBLICATIONS
185 WILLOW STREET • PO BOX 180 • MYSTIC, CT 06355
TEL: 1-800-321-0411 • FAX: 1-800-572-0788
E-MAIL: ttpubs@aol.com • www.twentythirdpublications.com
Bayard

*The church mice illustrations
are by Mark Hakomaki*

Twenty-Third Publications
A Division of Bayard
185 Willow Street
P.O. Box 180
Mystic, CT 06355
(860) 536-2611
(800) 321-0411
www.twentythirdpublications.com

ISBN:1-58595-308-3
Library of Congress Catalog Card Number: 2003113305
Printed in the U.S.A.

TABLE OF CONTENTS

ACKNOWLEDGMENTS

If Vatican II made one thing clear to us Catholics,
    it's that the reform of the Church,
    in all its dimensions and ministries,
        is ongoing.
Blessed Pope John XXIII said it best, I think,
    when he observed a need to examine ourselves closely
    and reform ourselves continuously
        because "all that the Gospel demands of us
        has not yet been fully revealed."
God is still speaking,
    still guiding and inspiring and aiding our ministry.

Throughout the United States and Canada,
    diocesan and parish leaders have been deeply involved
    with the ongoing reform of catechesis.
There are so many, it's hard to list them all.
But each one contributes to the overall growth of this ministry
    in the Church.
Each one brings experiments that worked, or didn't.
    Each brings ideas,
        hopes,
        and faith to the reform of catechesis.
Call it by whatever name you like,
    catechesis for the whole community
    is part of this reform.
Where once we were content to provide it for the youngsters,
    now we see we must provide it for all the People of God.

Thanks to all of you.
    All of you who have worked so hard in this ministry,
    innovated so creatively,
    and been so patient when the results were slow in coming sometimes.
Thanks to those who pioneered the renewal of the catechumenate.
    First and foremost, that is what shapes the Church today
        around the world.

It's shaping catechesis in new ways
    in the United States and Canada as well.
Thanks to those who worked so diligently
    with the revised lectionary after the Council,
    providing catechesis based on,
        or connected to,
        the Liturgy of the Word.
Thanks to those who experimented and tested
    family and household based catechesis,
    to those who have been developing intergenerational approaches,
    and to those who have produced two or three generations
        of fine children's textbooks.

And of course, thanks to all of you who work in this ministry.
    You have been heroines and heroes.
You have worked so many long hours,
    so many evenings and weekends,
    and at such low rates of pay most of the time.
You have consistently been willing to grow,
    to try something new,
    to reform the way we work in catechesis.
The diocesan level leaders are important to the Church,
    but it's the parish workers who are
    on the front lines of this ministry.
        Hats off to you all!

Many of you have had a hand
    in the preparation of this handbook.
    It's dedicated to you.

In the Diocese of Trenton,
    remember how we sat together looking out at the ocean that week
    and talked from top to bottom
    about how we could expand catechesis
        to include the whole community?
Chick McGinty is the one who called us all together,
    but Marty Arsenault and Eileen Hoefling were part of the leadership, too.
We shared meals and liturgy and yes,
    even a little wine maybe.
A lot of good came out of that.
    Much of it is in this handbook now.

In the Diocese of Raleigh,
    I remember more than once how we all came together

and put our shoulders to the wheel
   to try to understand how best to announce the Good News today.
It was hot in Raleigh that week,
   but we trudged on,
   taking short breaks and working darn hard.
We decided that week regarding how to refer to this in Spanish,
   Catequesis para toda la Comunidad.
   Remember that?
It was Jan Vallero who convened that meeting,
   but Rob Jones and Mike Hagarty were front and center, too.
I came home with a dozen pages of notes
   from the discussions we held together.
   You'll find them in this handbook.

And how about you folks in Los Angeles?
   Edith Prendergast and the whole staff there
   could see very early on
   that the *General Directory* was serious
      in calling for us to move beyond
      a children-only program of catechesis
      to an approach intended for the whole community.
Frank Montejano called all the school leaders and religion departments together
   almost two full years ago already.
And Steven Ellair has led the way
   with the parish religious education programs.
Remember all those meetings,
   first up in the San Fernando Valley,
   then down in the San Pedro region,
   then out in the San Gabriel area,
      and on and on?
(How did LA get to be so darn big?)
The contributions of all those wonderful, dedicated leaders
   are reflected here in this handbook.

Long ago in the city of Dubuque, Iowa,
   the leaders of all the parishes and schools,
   and there are nine or ten of them in Dubuque,
   came together to start exploring what it would mean
      to adopt an approach more aimed at the whole community.
They could plainly see the need
   and they were searching for ways.
Remember how you patiently worked through the principles involved
   and some of the earliest ideas
   about how to implement this?

I have to give credit for much of that to Sr. Marilyn Breen,
   to Loretta Ryan,
   to Sr. Marci Blum
      but to so many more there!
It spread from Dubuque to Waterloo
   and then to the rest of the Archdiocese!
Their very practical questions,
   their willingness to wrestle with the details
   were a first impetus to develop this handbook.

And then there is Chicago.
   Pat Reddington on the parish catechesis side
   and David Beaudoin (who's now in Providence) on the schools side
      led the way.
Remember that summer when we spent all those days
   talking through the theology
   and the obstacles
   and the possibilities for change?
What I remember best about that
   is the hope I saw in Chicago that summer.
There was bad news on the wires
   about Church leadership,
   but you would never have known it.
Those people were simply dedicated
   to finding a way to renew the Church
   and help more people come to Christ.
Maruja Sedano is there now as director at the ORE.
And Esther Hicks has picked up the ball in the schools office.
   How lucky can Chicago get?

In the Diocese of Albany,
   Jeanne Schrempf, always a leader,
   could see early on that it was time for renewal.
Remember that huge meeting we held last year?
I was so touched by the complete dedication
   and especially by the desire
   of both the parish and diocesan leaders
   to renew our ministry and broaden it
      to include the whole community.
Jeanne was the leader,
   but David Amico,
   Sr. Pat Conron,
      and all the rest were on board, too.
I'm hearing good things about the work in Albany these days.

A lot of faith is being shared there,
and many are coming to catechesis.
Good for you!

And then there was that exciting group in the State of Kentucky.
Remember that statewide directors' meeting in Louisville two years ago?
Wow!
All four dioceses, working together,
sharing a vision,
moving forward.
What a tribute to our ministry you are!
Matt Hayes and Sue Grenough from Louisville,
Sr. Stella over in Covington,
Patty Blair in Owensboro,
and Pat Guentert in Lexington.
(I might remember that so well
partly because they sent me home
with a bottle of Maker's Mark.)
But isn't that a fine group of leaders in a single state?
Look for good things to come from Kentucky.
Their ideas and hopes are reflected here in this handbook.

Remember in Metuchen,
how we gathered in that old seminary meeting hall for a day together,
and spent it getting ourselves excited
about the possibility of shifting gears
and creating an approach to catechesis for the parish
that would offer the whole community a chance to renew its faith?
It was Mary Kay Cullinan leading the charge there.
Mary Kay was an early advocate of a wider approach
and her influence in this handbook is tremendous.

And in Greensburg, meeting out at the Abbey,
remember how we wrestled with all those practical questions:
budgets,
being overworked already,
finding willing participants,
and all the rest?
I have to give you credit.
You raised the tough issues.
But even more credit to you and Sr. Joan Supel
for diving in and seeking a better way.
I hope some of those tough issues are being resolved
and I hope this handbook helps.

Oh, and down in Evansville,
    remember how we marched through those two days together,
    first with the parish folks and then with the diocesan staff?
There were many pastors there that week and good for them.
    Like the rest of us,
    they're working hard and it can be tough to find time
    to sit around and dream about reform.
But isn't that the work we must do?
Sr. Geraldine Hedinger called that meeting,
    and her assistant, Donna Gish, was part of the process,
    along with Bob Cox.
Some fine ministry is happening in Evansville.

And then there was that rainy morning in Rockville Center,
    up in that odd back room of the old restaurant.
    Remember that?
The number was small because it was a busy time of year.
    But the enthusiasm was large.
And there were many people there already experimenting
    with ways to involve more of the whole community.
Sr. Ann Marie Dean and George Rand have been leading that charge.

And how about those folks in Charleston,
    Paul Schroeder leading the way.
Remember that lovely day we had together up in Columbia?
You know better than most the challenge of providing catechesis
    in an environment that is so ecumenical and so rural!
We really tackled the nuts and bolts that day, didn't we?
Much of what we did then
    is in this handbook.

In Winona, Mark Nuerhing has had this vision for a long time,
    even before he got to his present job.
What great leadership he's bringing to this!
    That diocese has already held workshops
    presented by parishes within the diocese
    sharing actual models and ways to broaden catechesis
        to the whole community.
Every diocese will soon be there!

This list is deficient in that it leaves off so many others
    who are leading the way:
    Anne Comeaux in Galveston-Houston,
    Jim Corr in Omaha,

Dennis Beeman in Richmond,
JoAnne Dalhoff in Des Moines,
Mary Wieser and Pat Finan in Davenport,
Peg Ruble in Charlotte,
all the directors in the state of California,
    Sr. Olive Murphy in Santa Rosa,
    Sr. Jeannine Leichner in San Jose,
    Ruth Bradley in Orange,
    Bob Melevin in San Bernardino,
    Sr. Celeste Arbuckle in San Francisco,
    Marc Gonzalez in Oakland
    Ginger Infantio in San Diego
        and all the others...

Lee Nagel has been identifying this need in Green Bay
    for as long as I can remember,
Dan John in Salt Lake City,
Sr. Clarissa up in Boise,
Roger Cadotte in Superior,
John Meyer in Phoenix,
Carol Augustine in Baltimore, who has given herself to this
    for most of her life,
Jack McBride in Madison
    who's been a leader on this for a decade,
Jim Kemna and Carolyn Saucier in Jefferson City,
Dennis Johnson in Grand Rapids,
Jo Ann Borchert in New Ulm,
Bro Ed, Richard Cheri, Len Enger, and Ken Richard
    in New Orleans,
Sr. Linda Gaupin in Orlando,
    a strong believer in renewing the whole community,
Deacon James over in Palm Beach
    committed to this vision,
Maribeth Mancini and the whole staff up in Rochester,
Sr. Katie Eiffe down the road in Syracuse,
Ellie Krupa in San Antonio,
Sr. Lucy Clynes in St. Augustine,
Sharon Horgan in Minneapolis-St. Paul and her staff
    and all those parishes in ACRE there,
Brian Lemoi of course, in St. Petersburg,
and Ed Gordon in Wilmington,
    who along with Cathy Minkiewicz of Boston and others
    have been calling for an expansion to adult formation
        for ten years,

Sr. Rosa Monique Pena in Miami has developed actual models,
Kathy Kleinlein down in Venice,
    and, well,
      this list could go on and on...

I haven't even mentioned the national leadership in
    NCEA,
    NPCD,
    NCCL,
    and all the rest,
nor have I mentioned the international leadership
    coming from folks like Joanne Chafe
    of the Canadian Bishops' Conference.

I haven't mentioned the many publishers
    who are committed to this renewal,
    Pascal Ruffenach, Gwen Costello, and Mary Carol Kendzia
      at Twenty-Third Publications,
    Diane Lampitt and the staff at Harcourt Religion Publishers,
    Maryann Nead at RCL where the whole community
      was a focus of product development
      a full decade ago in the Vatican II Center,
    Cullen Schippe at Benziger, who was an early leader.
    Other publishers, too, are stepping up to the plate.

I haven't mentioned the writers
    who are contributing so much to this movement
    toward the whole community.
These are the unseen ones who prepare the manuscripts
    for textbooks,
    trade books,
    and other educational materials.
      Hats off to you!

Nor have I mentioned Tim Ragan
    at the East Coast Conference
    who has always believed in this
or John Roberto at the Center for Ministry Development
    who is providing very creative leadership right now.

Nor have I mentioned the university and college community
    now beginning to offer courses
    that aim at helping students prepare for this ministry,
      in the whole community:

Jane Regan at Boston College tops the list,
    and Michael Moran at Loyola Marymount in LA,
    followed by others such as
        Brian Schmisek at the University of Dallas,
        Mark Markuly and Butch Eckstrom
            at the LIMEX program at Loyola of the South
            and others...
And of course, the list of leaders at the parish level
    is just too long to even start mentioning by name.
But you get the point.

One person I do have to mention by name is Jo Rotunno.
She has a deep grasp of the need
    for a comprehensive and systematic method
    with which to shift these gears
        from children only to whole community.
She understands well that we must connect what we do
    to the lectionary and the Sunday Assembly.
And she is a realist about parish life,
    having been there herself once upon a time.
What we're talking about in this book won't be easy.
It's going to require that another whole generation of leaders
    agree to put their shoulders to the wheel
        and work very hard.
But renewal is never easy.
    It always comes with a cost.
Jo was a big help to me in all the ways I just cited
    as I prepared these notes to be published.
Her new book, *Heritage of Faith:*
    A Framework for Catechesis in the Whole Community
    is absolutely excellent.
It lays the groundwork every parish will need to proceed
    with a process that involves the whole community.

And one other influential person who must be mentioned by name
    is Mark Hakomaki.
Mark is the artist who provides us
    with the church mice drawings we see here
    and have seen before elsewhere.
They're not just some accidental addition to this text.
They help us loosen our ties or neck scarves,
    unlace our shoes,
    lighten up a little,
        and see our work as humorous and fun.

We tend to take it all so seriously
    and, indeed, we do serious work!
But Mark gives us the special gift of humor.
He sees the world as divine gift,
    and he never hesitates to stop,
    in the middle of the busiest day,
        to tell the name of a particular plant,
        or to see what fragrance that flower has,
        or to laugh at a silly thing,
        or to make romantic what is otherwise merely mundane.
That gift for making things romantic
    is the same gift as making them loving and kind.
It emerges from the heart of the gospel
    and is a marvelous vision
    which these church mice also convey.
When you reproduce these pages for use in your parish,
    reproduce the church mice with them.
Everyone who gets the handouts will be grateful.

Emily Dickinson is a heroine of mine.
I liked her quirky independence there in Amherst
    where she lived.
She published books herself
    and she didn't like it any more than I do.
To me, publishing is like buying a computer.
    By the time this gets into print,
    I'm sure I will have revised some of my thinking,
    learned another lesson from one of those people mentioned above,
    or realized I was downright wrong about something.
Emily Dickinson once said that publishing a book
    is like taking your pants down in public.
    It exposes you.

But I think we have to do this
    and I encourage you to do it, too.
Take those notes you've got,
    shape them up a bit,
    and share them with the rest of us!
        We're in a period of important renewal here.
        Vatican II is still being implemented.
        There's a lot to do and we need all hands on deck.

INTRODUCTION

The signs that guide us for catechesis

We get our understanding of catechesis
    in today's Church
    from two sources:
        good, old common sense,
            which arises
            out of our shared experience,
    and Church documents,
        which arise in part
        from recent papal teaching.
These two sources are closely related.
    Church teaching is drawn from common sense
    and common sense comes from the experience
        of working under Church teaching.
We draw on both of these sources
    as we peer into our own times
    to read them as well as we can,
        to trust them and see in them
        the signs that guide us for catechesis.

"The signs of our times"
    rise out of what's happening around us:
        the politics of war-making
            and its link to corporate interests
            in so many governments,
        climate change on a global scale,
        the desire for peace in the hearts of so many,
        the growing number of materially poor,
        the changing roles of women,
        the shift in who makes up a household,
        new waves of immigrants,
        a pervasive media presence,
        a much less dominantly Christian
            and more multi-faith world,

materialism and consumerism as social values,
decreasing Catholic identity
in much more ecumenical households,
less and less respect for human dignity
in the face of
genocide,
poverty,
refugee migrations,
and loss of human rights,
a growing sense of world community
linked to the use of the Internet
and shared ideas and values.

In listing the signs of our times,
we do not mean to suggest
that the list contains "bad" or "good" items,
as much as to discover within our times
signals that can lead us to
freedom,
peace,
shared wealth,
and comfort for all.

Given these signs of our times,
how can we provide
a clear and compelling process by which
Christians can grow in their faith?
How can we aid those folks who wish
to follow Christ
and help them become
"salt" within their communities?
How can we help these committed Christians
come to understand that God is merciful,
that Christ empowers us for love,
that we share responsibility for the world,
and that all humans are our sisters and brothers?
How can we help the many baptized
but uncommitted Christians
consider their faith a priority
and source of values,
strength,
and happiness?

The General Directory for Catechesis

The real basis of our thinking lies mainly
in the *General Directory for Catechesis* (GDC).
This document was called for in Rome
    by the bishops at Vatican II,
    written over a span of more than three decades,
    the result of worldwide consultation and input,
    based solidly on papal teaching,
        Vatican II's insights,
        and Scripture itself.
    Finally it was signed by Pope John Paul II,
        translated into all the world's languages,
        and sent to every diocese.
In consulting this amazing document
    we see that it, too, seeks
    to read the signs of the times
    and the state of catechesis in the Church,
        and to bring them together.
The GDC advises us,
    cajoles us,
    points us in the right direction,
    and affirms our own common sense.
It is our guide,
    indeed, *the* guide for all we do
    in catechesis in today's Church.
From it we can draw certain principles
    for catechesis in today's world.
These principles, in turn,
    will shape the processes we develop
    at the parish and school
    and even at the household level of the Church.

What this handbook provides

Chapter one explores these seven principles in detail.
    Reproducible master pages are also provided
        to teach these principles to others.
        These masters include reflection questions
            for use within the parish.
With them, you can lead fruitful discussions
    among your leaders
    as a way of entering into these new ideas
        with grace and unity.

Chapter two takes another step
    by exploring another important document,
    published by the bishops of the U.S.,
        Our Hearts Were Burning Within Us.
The Leader's Guide to this document
    is packed with suggestions and resources
    to help you make adult catechesis
        the norm in your community.
This chapter suggests nine ways you can get started
    within your own parish or school.

Chapter three shifts gears
    and leaps headlong into the nuts and bolts
    of whole community catechesis.
The first step, of course,
    is to provide opportunities in your parish
    through which folks can meet Christ,
        renew their faith in Christ,
        and deepen their commitment;
        in short, ways they can experience ongoing conversion.
This handbook provides two avenues for that.
First, you'll find a well-tested,
    parish-based retreat program
    called Living with Christ.
This handbook provides reproducible master pages
    to help you launch this program in your parish.
Second, you'll find the tools you need
    for parish-wide faith sharing.
Faith sharing is essential in parish life;
    it's how we meet Christ,
    share Christ with others,
    and experience ongoing conversion,
        one of the key themes of the GDC.
This handbook includes a guide to help you
    launch faith sharing in your parish and school;
    this guide is provided as a reproducible master.
Such sharing might be based on Questions of the Week
    for each cycle of the lectionary.

Chapter four provides a resource
    you will find nowhere else,
    two tools which will be
        of enormous help in your parish.
First, we provide you with a brief statement

explaining why it's so important
for us in the Church
to follow a comprehensive
and systematic course
when teaching about the faith.
This is presented here in reproducible format
so you can easily share it with others.

Second, we provide you with the rationale
and outline
to help you develop a scope and sequence
for your whole community.
A "scope and sequence," as you know,
is a framework,
a skeleton outline
which, when followed,
will provide a full treatment
on the faith.
It would be difficult for each parish
to develop one of these for itself,
which is why we are outlining ideas for one here.
Our suggestions for this will result in an adult focus
for instructions in the faith
connected to the lectionary used at Mass on Sundays.
This lectionary-connected approach
results in a unified parish process:
the Sunday assembly
connected to all catechesis,
connected to pastoral care,
connected to other prayer and worship,
connected to work for justice and peace.
On this framework, as you will see,
you can hang all your catechesis for adults,
making adult catechesis the norm
rather than a sideline to the children's program.
The resources you will need to deliver the catechesis
called for in this scope and sequence
are provided by a variety of publishers.
They include things such as
bulletin inserts, brief treatments of theology,
certain books presented in plain English,
selected web sites, magazines,
pamphlets and booklets,
and others.

Chapter five is a practical guide for catechetical gatherings.
Whether you plan to continue to use classrooms
     for religious instruction
     or shift to catechesis assemblies,
          this guide will help you.
It provides suggestions to for developing
     more meaningful religion sessions
     connected to the whole community.
Chapter five outlines and shares information
     about catechesis assemblies,
     those wonderful gatherings
          of children,
          youth,
          adults,
          or all of the above.
These assemblies are a fine way for your parish
     to provide catechesis
     in a context that feels more like Church
          than it does school.
Getting them organized
     and carrying them off well
     is the business of chapter five.
This chapter is filled with reproducible master pages
     so that you can share with others in your parish.

Chapter six is a short guide
     on how to send religion home.
If we are learning anything at all
     in these days of growth and development
     in light of the GDC,
          it's that the goal of catechesis
          is to develop households of faith.
The most fantastic parish process for catechesis,
     no matter how "whole community" it is,
     will fail unless the households in the parish
          become little domestic churches.
That's how important homemaking is
     to the Church.
This chapter provides you with a practical guide
     as you consider ways to do this.
Working together,
     we will succeed in deepening faith
     and building the Church
          one household at a time.

Chapter seven provides you
        with several "short courses"
        which you can use in your bulletin,
                or print as a single flier
                to help folks understand
                about whole community catechesis.
Being clear about whole community catechesis,
        sharing information freely with all,
        communicating over and over again,
                is what will make you successful.
We have said several times here
        that *language creates reality*.
If you call your catechetical process
        by a name that sounds
        like a children's program,
                then you'll have only a children's program.
But if you call it by a name
        that suggests everyone is invited,
        everyone is welcome,
        everyone is expected to be in catechesis,
                then over time
                an adult focus will emerge.

Use the short courses in chapter seven over and over again
        in committee meetings;
        in training events;
        any way you wish.
You may reprint them
        without any further permission from us.

In conclusion

Thank you for all you do for catechesis
in your own parish or school.
Every time I visit a diocese or parish,
every time I take part in a workshop
at a regional or national conference,
I am deeply impressed by the commitment
of men and women like you and me.
The Church depends on us,
leaders,
catechists,
participants,
all of us.
It depends on us to echo the faith
in our own lives
and to lead others to Christ.
Thank you for taking up this work
with such good heart
and solid faith.

CHAPTER ONE

The Seven Principles of Whole Community Catechesis

■ *Principle #1:*
Catechesis has several tasks

When we begin to think about catechesis
      as it's described in the *General Directory for Catechesis*
      (which we often call, simply, the GDC),
      some of us may be tempted
            to equate catechesis
            with religious instruction.
We may think that catechesis is merely
      a new name
      for what we've always done
            in our religious ed programs.
But in fact, the GDC is clear in saying
      that there's much more to catechesis
      than what we do in religious instruction.
Religious instruction is one dimension—
      an important one
      but not the only dimension—
            of catechesis
            as we are now coming to understand it.
Such instruction can assist in faith development
      by helping the learner to understand
      the Christian message more fully.
Religious instruction is the part of catechesis
      on which we can "test" the outcomes.
We can evaluate how much a learner knows
      about the sacraments,
      Church history,
      the rites,
      doctrines,
      and moral teachings of the Church.
We can give grades and scores.
We can even pass or fail a child
      on his or her grasp
      of the facts.
A systematic presentation of the faith,
      in age-appropriate language
      with a proper textbook,
            and found to be in conformity
            with the *Catechism of the Catholic Church*,
            is very important.

The bishops have asked
>   everyone working in the ministry of catechesis
>   to provide such a comprehensive presentation
>>   to anyone who comes forward
>>   asking to learn about the faith.
In the United States,
>   Catholic textbook publishers
>   have stepped up to the plate on this
>>   and hit a home run!
The books are generally well-written,
>   comprehensive,
>   and systematic.
They cover the facts,
>   along with liturgy,
>>   prayer,
>>   education for community life,
>>   and family connections.

Yet there is a tendency,
>   perhaps more in the United States
>   than in some other parts of the world,
>>   to reduce catechesis
>>   to the one dimension
>>   of religious instruction.
We are absolutely intent on following
>   an educational framework
>   for religious education
>>   that resembles and mimics
>>   how we teach other subjects.
We use a framework for providing catechesis
>   which is sometimes called
>   the "schoolhouse framework"
>   because that's precisely what it is.

We sometimes think that if only the learners
>   get the facts down right,
>   they'll grow up to be
>   adult Christians of mature faith.
Of course,
>   deep down we know that's not enough,
>   and that there's much more to do.

The *General Directory for Catechesis*
   agrees wholeheartedly.
In articles 85 and 86, the GDC tells us
   that the fundamental tasks of catechesis include:
      (1) promoting knowledge of the faith,
            which is what we call religious instruction;
      (2) liturgical education,
            leading to a true liturgical life;
      (3) moral formation,
            learning to follow the Way
            based on conversion to Jesus Christ;
      (4) teaching to pray,
            which requires apprenticeship;
      (5) education for community life,
            including the ecumenical dimension;
      (6) development of households of faith;
      (7) preparation to work in the vineyard
            as an active minister
            in an interfaith setting.
      (8) Over and above all this, according to the GDC,
            catechesis also must be grounded first
            in conversion to Jesus Christ and his Way,
               and it must be something we live
               within our household, in everyday life!

Wow! That's quite a job description!
Every leader in catechesis,
   especially at the parish level,
   must be reeling as they wonder
      how they'll ever shift gears in present programs
         to broaden the scope for this work.
In the past we've been able to organize
   a *program* for the first task,
   "promoting knowledge of the faith,"
      but now we're called to go much further.
This is the first principle that flows from the GDC:
   catechesis has many dimensions.
It includes religious education
   but goes much further,
   demanding a full process of formation
      for each learner.
In this respect,
   catechesis as envisioned in the GDC
   resembles what happens in the catechumenate.

■ FOR PARISH REFLECTION

How does this wider view of catechesis
    fit into your own understanding?
Which of these eight tasks
    seems most challenging to you?
Using the Tasks of Catechesis Worksheet on the next page,
    rate how your present program
    addresses each of these tasks.

Tasks of Catechesis Worksheet

TASKS from the GDC, #s 85 & 86	RATE HOW YOU'RE DOING NOW from 1 = not well at all to 9 = very well	LIST WAYS BY WHICH YOU MIGHT MAKE THIS MORE OF A PRIORITY
1. Promoting knowledge of the faith, which is what we call "religious instruction"	1 2 3 4 5 6 7 8 9 Explain	
2. Liturgical education, leading to a true liturgical life	1 2 3 4 5 6 7 8 9 Explain	
3. Moral formation, learning to follow the Way of Christ, based on conversion to Jesus	1 2 3 4 5 6 7 8 9 Explain	
4. Teaching to pray, which requires apprenticeship	1 2 3 4 5 6 7 8 9 Explain	
5. Education for community life, including the ecumenical dimension	1 2 3 4 5 6 7 8 9 Explain	
6. The development of households of faith	1 2 3 4 5 6 7 8 9 Explain	
7. Preparation to work in the vineyard as an active minister in an interfaith setting	1 2 3 4 5 6 7 8 9 Explain	
8. Catechesis grounded first in conversion to Jesus Christ and his Way—something we live within our households, in everyday life	1 2 3 4 5 6 7 8 9 Explain	

Principle #2:
Catechesis is constitutive of the Christian life

The term "constitutive"
  can put people off.
Its meaning is not clear to everyone,
    but it is such an important word
    that a brief definition is in order here.
Simply put, it means
    that catechesis in all its dimensions,
        is part and parcel of the Christian life.
Catechesis is essential,
    not just for kids
    but for all Christians
    of every age and state in life;
        it's not optional.
You can't really consider yourself
    a follower of Jesus Christ
        unless you grow daily
        to be more fully faithful.
We don't realize the reign of God
    all at once
    but gradually, as we grow in our faith.
Faith is a lifelong journey,
    not a once-and-for-all agreement.

Being in the Sunday assembly each week
    is also constitutive.
For that reason, the Church has always
    considered it gravely sinful
    to be absent from the Sunday assembly.
By gravely sinful we mean that a pattern of absence
    from the grace of the Mass
    renders our hearts poorer.
It creates a situation in our lives
    where we are "going it alone."
And going it alone is not how we reach
    the heart of the Lord.
We come to the Lord together,
    bound by one inner Source:
        the Spirit.

By assembling with each other,
    by celebrating the great mysteries,
    by sharing in communion,
    by breaking open the Word,
        we "go it together,"
        which is how we become whole.

Catechesis is just like this;
    we can't learn about our faith alone.
We can't grow and prosper
    unless we do so with others
        in our community.

Likewise, working for justice and peace
    is constitutive of the Christian life.
The Christian faith is not something
    merely intellectual.
It is more than an assent of the mind
    to certain doctrinal truths.
For this reason, the GDC makes it clear
    that part of catechesis is preparing
    to live as a Christian.
What does it mean to live as Jesus did?
Even a casual glance through the gospels
    will show you that it means
    to "bring glad tidings to the poor,
        to proclaim liberty to captives,
        and recovery of sight to the blind,
        to let the oppressed go free" (Lk 4:18).
It means to give food to the hungry,
    and drink to the thirsty,
    to welcome strangers,
    clothe the naked,
    care for the ill,
    and visit the imprisoned (Mt 25).
Living as Jesus did means to love our enemies,
    to give alms without drawing attention,
    to pray in private,
    and to build up treasure in heaven (Mt 5 and 6).

It means to have homes ready for guests,
    to share supper often,
    and to find in those moments
        that Christ is present there (Lk 16, 19, 24).
We cannot really say
    that we are faithful followers of Christ
    unless we live in justice and peace.

These three actions, then—
    participating in catechesis,
    working for justice and peace,
    and participating in the Sunday assembly—
        are part and parcel of being Christian.
They're lifelong processes,
    and they're part of our great shared legacy.

So whatever program of faith formation
    you follow in your parish for the children
        must now extend to the whole community.
The scope and sequence of the textbooks you use
    must reach beyond children.
    You must be able to reach people
        of all ages and backgrounds
        within the parish.

■ FOR PARISH REFLECTION

If you were going to prepare

    a whole community scope and sequence
    for your parish and school,
    what would be your first three steps?
Who would do this work?
    Who would support it?
    Who would object?
Using the outline for a scope and sequence
    in *Heritage of Faith* by Jo Rotunno
    plan a one-season process of catechesis
        for your whole community.

Principle #3:
Conversion precedes catechesis

If you read it carefully,
    the *General Directory* might seem
    preoccupied with conversion.
By conversion, it simply means
    turning our hearts to Christ
    over and over again
        throughout our lives.
Turning our hearts,
    making Christ the center,
    focusing on the Way of Christ:
        this is what must happen
        before catechesis is possible.
We often rush headlong into catechesis—
    concerned that every learner
    grasp the doctrine and content well
        without allowing time for conversion.
Conversion as we are describing it here
    does not normally have a place
    within traditional religious education programs
    in the United States.
Many assume that knowing the doctrinal definitions
    is the same
    as knowing Christ.
While knowing doctrine can help deepen faith
    and express the experience of Christ,
    it is not, by itself, the same as meeting Christ,
        turning our hearts to Christ,
        and living what we believe.

However, the GDC is very clear:
    "many who present themselves for catechesis
    truly require genuine conversion" (#62).
For this reason, the GDC goes on to say,
    the Church desires that
    "the first stage in the catechetical process
        be dedicated to ensuring conversion."

The reason for this concern about conversion
    is that the business of catechesis
    is all about coming to know and walk
        with Christ
        in our daily lives.
Jesus Christ is the first and last point of reference
    in catechesis,
    according to the *Catechism of the Catholic Church* (CCC, #1698).
According to St. Paul,
    for us, to live is Christ (Phil 1:21).
Jesus not only is the Word of God
    but also transmits that Word (GDC, #98).
There is no doubt about this:
    we must find in our lives
    opportunities for conversion,
        for turning our hearts to Christ
        over and over again.
These opportunities might include retreat experiences,
    breaking open the Word,
    engaging in works of justice or charity,
    faith sharing,
    or others.

The GDC uses a term
    to describe this process
    of coming to conversion.
It calls it *evangelization*.
For Catholics, this is a new word
    but an important one.
It refers to that basic step
    we all must take
    over and over again throughout life
        in which we respond to God's invitation.
God invites us to ever deeper faith
    through the Good News of Scripture,
    through the liturgy of the Church,
    through shared meals in our homes,
    through the needs of the poor and rejected,
    through the ongoing teaching of the Church,
    through all of creation,
    through the direct witness of others,
        the love of our spouses or friends
        the sharing of our faith
        and many other ways.

In all these ways,
    we are *evangelized*,
    we are called to life in Christ.
When we respond
    we turn our hearts to God.
That is conversion.
Persons involved in youth ministry
    can teach us a great deal about this.
They are concerned that,
    before formal education occurs,
    the young people first meet Christ,
    turn their hearts to Christ,
    and begin to live as young Christians.
Using experiences such as Search weekends,
    Teens Encounter Christ weekends,
    or other retreat experiences,
        the focus is on conversion
        as a first step.
Youth ministers have something to teach the rest of us,
    and many elements of their approach
    can be found in whole community catechesis.

■ FOR PARISH REFLECTION

This will be a more personal sharing
    than we have done with other principles.
What is your own experience
    of meeting Christ in your life,
    of turning your heart to Christ,
    of deepening your friendship with Christ,
    and of letting Christ touch your daily life?

Principle #4:
All catechesis is tightly connected to the Sunday assembly

"Catechesis," Pope John Paul II wrote (*Catechesis Tradendae*, #23)
    "is intrinsically bound to every liturgical
        and sacramental action."
We really can't do catechesis
    outside the context of the Church's liturgical life.
Likewise, good liturgy demands good catechesis.
    But how do we link these two?

The *General Directory* advises us
    to use the catechumenate as our model
    when planning for catechesis (#90-91).
By this it does not mean to suggest
    that catechesis
    has to be an exact replica of the RCIA.
That really wouldn't be feasible
    since we'd have to dismiss everyone
    after the homily each weekend.
But we can take elements of the catechumenate,
    ancient, sacred practices used there,
    and incorporate them into catechesis.
One of the first elements we will need to adopt
    is breaking open the Word.

Simply put, in breaking open the Word
    those in catechesis pause
        to consider the readings of Scripture
        from the Sunday assembly.
They reread them,
    pray over them,
    and share their faith about them.
By sharing their faith openly this way,
    they experience a turning of their hearts,
        a conversion to Christ.
This conversion leads to a desire
    to understand Christ and their faith more deeply
    and to allow their lives to be touched more profoundly.
This desire to understand their faith
    and make it part of their lives
    is what leads to a *desire for catechesis*.

This *desire for catechesis*
        is precisely what is lacking in most young people
        in our faith formation programs
        and in nearly every adult in the Church today.
Again, the desire for catechesis arises from conversion;
        it cannot be forced onto anyone.
This desire is the direct work of the Holy Spirit
        as our hearts are open to God's action by faith.
To sum it up, by breaking open the Word
        Christians of all ages can experience profound conversion
                over and over again,
                day in and day out,
        and this conversion leads to catechesis.

Whole community catechesis, therefore,
        is less committed to "lectionary based" catechesis
        and more committed to "lectionary *connected*" catechesis.
A lectionary *based* program
        derives all teachings of the Christian faith
        from Scripture—with only an eye to Tradition.
Instead, a lectionary *connected* program
        derives teachings about the faith
        from Scripture and Tradition
        and *connects* it all to the liturgy.
In this way, the liturgy holds pride of place
        in the process.
It's the true fountain of everything else that occurs
        in catechesis
        or the life of the parish.
But how we do make this lectionary connection?
        How do we connect all catechesis
        to the Sunday assembly?
There are two avenues for this journey.
The first is a form of faith sharing
        or breaking open the Word
        or simple "checking in" with one another,
                done in light of the Sunday readings.

The second is more elusive
        but equally important.
Each parish must find a way to welcome everyone
        to the Sunday assembly,
and not just welcome them,
        but make everyone *feel* welcome:

make them feel important,
    wanted,
        a vital part of the community.
When I say everyone I mean *everyone*,
    even those normally excluded.
Unless every person feels welcome on Sunday,
    the work of catechesis
    will not proceed as it must.
If all are not included and welcomed,
    then those whom Christ himself most loved—
        the poor,
        the rejected,
        the sinner,
        the stranger, immigrant, and newcomer—
            will be ignored.
The gospel was originally preached to just such people,
    so how can we effectively witness to today's world
    unless all are welcome and present?

■ FOR PARISH REFLECTION

From part one of this principle:

    What are some ways in which you might
    connect your catechesis process
    to your Sunday assembly?
        What obstacles do you face
        in initiating faith sharing
        based on the Liturgy of the Word?

From part two of this principle:

    Who do you imagine feels most unwelcome
        in your Sunday assembly?
    Do you consider some people worthy
    and others unworthy to be present?
        Make up a list.
    How could you welcome these folks
        in Christ's name?

Principle #5:
The goal of all catechesis is to develop households of faith

For ministers of catechesis
    in parishes across the United States,
        this principle will be the hardest to swallow.
Yet all of us in this ministry agree that
    our task is not so much to build up programs
        at the parish or school level.
Our task is to help each household of the parish
    become a household of faith.
Faith must be lived in everyday life.
    It must be part and parcel
        of people's decisions,
            their hopes and dreams,
            their business and political activity,
            their contribution to the materially poor,
            their family life,
            and their supper table.
This latter place, the supper table,
    is perhaps the most important of all.
As we will see later in this handbook,
    supper is the memorial meal given to us by Christ.
It is the time when people connect with each other,
    when a certain group spirit sets in
        that heals and unites and supports us.

Faith is not something we do at the parish.
The Church does not live primarily at the parish level.
Our homes,
    our households
    are the places where we actually live
        what our catechesis teaches us.
All preaching is focused,
    and all our efforts for solid moral formation
        are aimed at life in the home.

Life at home is the immediate preparation
for celebrating the sacraments:
Eucharist,
reconciliation,
baptism,
matrimony,
and all the rest.

Homemaking is the process by which
you turn an ordinary house
into the place of comfort and security
that becomes a home.
It's the process by which a household
becomes a holy place in which to live,
by which it becomes "homey."

In the culture of every age,
there have been factors that supported home life,
and those that have worked against it.
However, regardless of the culture
and the economic situation
of the people living there,
families need to be serious
about *making a home.*
In fact, this is the very heart of everything
the Church tries to do.
No matter what church you belong to,
if you don't bring home
what is taught and done there,
then nothing you do at church matters either.
Why?
Because you don't live at church.
You live at home.

So homemaking is a vital part of life.
It's where everything comes together—
jobs,
faith,
recreation,
friendships,
illness,
wellness,
all of it.

Homemaking is important to everyone,
    but to people of faith
    it's even more important.

Catechesis, then, must always focus
    on developing life in the household.
All we do must be sent home.
We aren't in the ministry of catechesis
    to train young theologians,
    but to form folks in the faith
        so they can live by it.

■ FOR PARISH REFLECTION

What steps can you imagine taking
    as a parish community
    and in your catechetical process
        to be more effective in developing
        households of faith?
What obstacles must be overcome?
What resources do you need most?

Principle #6:
Catechesis must look and feel more like Church and less like school

As we've said above,
> much of the catechesis
> offered in the United States
> looks more like general curriculum schooling
> > than it looks like Church.

This poses a particular challenge.
Let me describe this just a little more for you,
> to help paint a picture of our starting point.

In most (but not all) parishes in America,
> religious education is provided
> using a framework or approach
> that follows a school format.

In this framework,
> children are enrolled
> in an optional program
> which follows the school year schedules,
> > formats,
> > and holidays.

In many places the families
> pay tuition for this program.

The children meet in classrooms,
> or, when there is no Catholic school,
> parishes often prepare makeshift meeting spaces
> to resemble those in a school.

The children are called students
> and their leaders are often called teachers.

The term *CCD teacher* is still common,
> despite efforts to change it to *catechist*.

The children use textbooks
> that resemble school texts,
> and the intent is mainly
> to present what is found in those books.

Parents are noticeably absent,
> just as in general curriculum schooling.

The work is done by volunteer parish catechists
> or homeroom teachers.

Most important, after about eighth grade or so,
    or after receiving the sacrament of confirmation,
    the children believe that they have graduated
    from religious education.
This sense of having graduated or finished their studies
    is very strong.
As a result, most post-confirmation
    or post-middle school faith formation programs
    are mainly youth activity programs
        of one kind or another.
Adult education is mainly left undone
    because most adults in the Church
    believe they have graduated
    from religious education which is,
        after all,
        for kids.

Anything that doesn't fit into this framework
    can't easily be added.
For example, a few years ago,
    the leaders in the movement
    to restore the catechumenate
    suggested a year-round schedule
    for the process of formation
    for candidates and catechumens.
        The main objection in practice
        was that this schedule would have to run over the summer,
        outside the school year calendar.
Most parish programs shut down for the summer.
In another example,
    many parishes have made fine attempts
    to provide adult education
    for their members.
However, these attempts have mainly been undertaken
    within the schoolhouse framework,
    consisting of a classroom setting,
    a presenter or teacher,
    a sense of being a student,
    and often even a textbook.
Even parish retreats or missions
    often occur within this framework.

The schoolhouse framework
  within which we provide religious education
  is common and pervasive.

Of course, there *is* a need
  for outright religious instruction
  so Christians can mature in their faith.
Understanding the sacred Scriptures,
  the Church's liturgies,
  its history,
  devotions,
  and doctrines
    is essential.
This is true for Christians of all age groups.
Our present schoolhouse framework
  does provide a structure
  within which this religious instruction
  is provided.
The textbooks are complete and beautiful.
  The students do seem to come away
  with a pretty good working knowledge of the Church.

However, here is what Steven Ellair,
  consultant for elementary catechesis
  in the Archdiocese of Los Angeles,
    noted about this:
"Our 'school-mode' applications
  of religious education
  also lead to more cognitively focused 'classrooms.'
This approach can lead to a de-emphasis
  on the affective and behavioral dimensions of learning
  and produce children who can recite prayers
    and Church doctrine,
    but who have little or no commitment to Church.
Intergenerational learning is by nature experiential and relational."

John Roberto, director of the Center for Ministry Development,
  noted in the introduction to his *Generations of Faith*
  a fine intergenerational model for catechesis:
"The current programmatic and age-specific approach
  to childhood and adolescent faith formation
  that has characterized the efforts of so many parishes
    over the past thirty years
    is simply not adequate.

It may be one of the models of faith formation in a parish,
     but it cannot be the only model.
It is time to broaden our vision and our practice."

Steven Ellair and John Roberto are correct.
     We need to seek new approaches
     that embrace the whole person
     and the whole community
        in faith formation.

Whole community catechesis
     assigns tremendous responsibility
     to the household of the learner.
It also remains a vital part of shared parish life,
     just as the Sunday assembly does.
In Pope John Paul II's teachings
     the parish remains the place
     where catechesis should occur
        in addition to the home.
In *Catechesi Tradendae,*
     his teaching on catechesis published in 1979,
     the pope has this to say,
"Catechesis always has been and always will be
     a work for which the whole Church
     must feel responsible
        and wish to be responsible."

■ FOR PARISH REFLECTION

What steps can you take
     to make your
     parish catechesis process
        feel more like Church
        and less like school?
How can you draw the families and households
     into the process,
     not as bystanders or guests
        but as regular participants?

Principle #7:
All catechesis builds on grace, which is offered to everyone

Grace is God's self-communication to us.
   God tells us about God's self in our innermost being,
   revealing who we are in the same process,
      and helping us become all we're created to be!
This same revealing God
   also communicates with us
      through the life of the Church:
      its ministers and leaders,
      its teachers and healers,
      its sacraments, symbols, and rites.
Grace is *experienced* as a divine, loving energy or power.

In his letter to the Colossians,
   when Paul is giving his own view
   of who he experiences Christ to be,
   he says that in Christ
      all things hold together.
God's grace is experienced like that:
   you feel yourself being empowered,
   filled up,
   prepared for a mission.
We know this grace
   comes from God alone
   and from no one else.
It's completely free,
   a truth so amazing that we have
      a hard time believing it.
   There is nothing we can do can
      to either earn or deserve
      God's grace.

What is truly miraculous is that grace
   is offered to every human being.
Every single person
   alive now or who ever lived
   is in God's hands.
Grace alone can make us whole.
   It lets us be precisely who we're made to be.

Grace is received and celebrated
    in community with each other,
    which is why we assemble
        for Eucharist,
        for catechesis,
        and for justice and peace.
We assemble in order to see more clearly,
    to hear better,
    and to work harder
        for God's reign on earth.

Uncreated grace is God's free and generous gift
    of God's self.
    It's sometimes called *sanctifying grace*.
Created grace is the effect in the human personality of that gift,
    and is sometimes called *actual grace*.
    Through actual grace God supports us in individual instances.

Grace is not an abstract theological notion.
    It fills our bodies and our souls
    and empowers us to love.
We are thus empowered to forgive,
    to accept without judgment,
    to give without asking for return,
    and to love without end.
This power can do marvelous things!
    It can heal and bind people together,
    give comfort and peace,
    offer affectionate love and help people grow,
    console the troubled and disturb the comfortable!
In a nutshell:
    grace is God's powerful force of love within us,
    planted by God and sustained by God.

This truth brings us to catechesis.

Those fifth graders in your group,
    those families in the assembly,
    those folks in the RCIA:
        God is already with them.
We don't bring God to people,
    we don't make God do things for people,
    we don't even direct how God behaves.

The plain truth is that
> God is acting in people's lives.

In light of that, our mission is
> to help people identify the experience of God
> in their lives.
>> Once they identify God's presence,
>> we can help them
>>> understand a little,
>>> celebrate a lot,
>>> and live forever in God's name.

That's about it.

That pretty much sums up the pastoral work
> of the Church.

Whole community catechesis is so important
> because this activity of God
> often goes without being acknowledged
>> or seen
>> or heard
>> or felt
>> or celebrated
>> or understood.

Yet, God's love is present throughout the community.

Just think of the power we have
> to assist in God's saving work
> as we help folks see this light
>> and live by it!

■ FOR PARISH REFLECTION

How can you make sure that God
> and God's surprising activity in our lives
> is not ignored
>> in your parish catechesis process?

As a way of experiencing this in your own lives,
> share your answers to these questions in your meeting:

What happened in my life
> in the past day or two
> that touched me or struck me as significant?

How was God's hand in that,
> or how did God seem absent?

CHAPTER TWO

Getting Started with Whole Community Catechesis

Nine suggestions to help you get started, based on *Our Hearts Were Burning Within Us*

Introduction

Responding in part
    to the new direction in catechesis
    suggested by the GDC,
        in 1999 the U.S. bishops
        published their own pastoral plan
        for adult catechesis
    under the title *Our Hearts Were Burning Within Us*.
They see the necessity of making adult formation
    a more vital priority
    for all members of the Church.
In article 6, they said:
    "We, as the Catholic bishops of the United States,
    call the Church in our country
    to a renewed commitment
    to *adult faith formation*,
        positioning it at the heart
        of our catechetical vision
            and practice." (italics are mine)
An excellent leader's guide for this pastoral plan
    was published recently
    and ought to be on every parish leader's desk.
It provides a means to implement the goals
    of the bishops' letter.

Writing in *Listening* in 1998,
    Jane Regan of Boston College said this:
    "Imagining an alternative vision of catechesis,
    one in which *the adult community* (italics are mine)
        is invited into the process of transformation,
        is the first step that needs to be taken
        as we move into the next millennium."
Jane Regan is right.
The first key is for you
    and other parish or school leaders
    to fire up your imaginations!
There is no one method with which to implement
    whole community catechesis.
Several excellent
    though different models are in use
    around the Church now.
So the first step is to imagine
    how this can work for you.
If you can imagine it, you can do it.

The second key is to have patience.
As you make the shift to whole community catechesis
    and implement *Our Hearts Were Burning Within Us,*
        your program may at first continue to look
            primarily like a children's catechetical program.
Indeed, most of the first participants
    in the catechesis assemblies or class sessions
    may be children.
But as the process of lifelong catechesis
    is modeled by the staff
    and encouraged within the whole community,
    more and more young people and adults
        will join the process.
The present children's program,
    with its staff and budget,
    will become the springboard for the whole community.

The third key is to *think communications!*
    Share the vision widely.
Start talking about whole community catechesis
    as a parish leadership group
    (pastor, staff, key volunteers,
        and leadership councils)
        as soon as possible.
Begin communicating with the whole parish
    early in the process.
Whenever a new idea is proposed,
    people will receive it very differently.
Some will immediately see the possible benefits
    and greater outcomes
    and be eager to move forward.
Others will be more cautious,
    worrying about how it will be received
    and wanting more time.
Still others will be loudly negative,
    seeing only the weaknesses,
        challenges,
        and pitfalls.
Before you start down this road,
    ask yourself how ready you are
    to handle all these responses.

Nine steps to get started

Here is a nine-step process that might help you.

1. Draw together the right folks for making a good decision.

2. Lay the groundwork within the parish for a solid beginning.

3. Get the parish started right away with faith sharing.

4. Begin a parish-based retreat process to deepen conversion.

5. Start preparing the whole community for the new approach.

6. Lay out a simple plan by which you will proceed.

7. Adjust parish schedules and budgets for the new approach.

8. As the process goes on, continue in the spirit of faith sharing.

9. Faithfully communicate the vision of whole community catechesis.

STEP 1. START WITH THE PARISH STAFF

You can't proceed without
    a *shared vision and desire*
    for whole community catechesis.
A prerequisite for this
    is that the staff already be committed to
    and inspired by
        the catechumenate.
Spend a couple of days over a month or so
    talking this through in detail
        with each other.

This handbook provides a ready-made
    discussion guide.
Each of the principles in chapter one
    is reproducible.
    All of those principles have reflection questions
        which can help you deepen your reflection
            as a staff or community.
You might want to draw into this conversation
    your various formation and education
    committees, commissions, or task forces.
Also, because this affects the renewal
    of the whole community,
    the principles would also be good material
        for pastoral council discussions.

Part of getting started, of course,
    is to choose a competent leader.
The leader is the one
    who sees the whole picture
    and helps communicate the vision and mission
        of a new idea.
The leader bears a lot of risk
    in leading the group and the parish
    forward toward a new goal.
Without that leader,
    every little obstacle raised
    will have the power to derail the process.
The leader has to champion the vision
    of whole community catechesis,
    helping others see how this new approach
    will benefit the whole parish
    even before he or she can grasp it all himself or herself.

The *Our Hearts Were Burning Within Us* Leader's Guide
    has excellent resources to help you
    develop leaders.

STEP 2. LAY THE GROUNDWORK

Once you decide as a parish community to proceed,
    lay the groundwork for whole community catechesis.
Prepare the whole parish community for this change.
Use the bulletin, the homily,
    notices and posters in the entries,
    and letters to each household.
Speak about it at every meeting of parishioners,
    no matter why they're gathering,
    from the ushers' meeting to the festival committee.
The notes in this handbook, along with the reproducible master pages,
    can be widely reprinted in your parish
    without any further permission.
This handbook contains several bulletin short courses
    to help you prepare the whole community
    for the activities of whole community catechesis.
Each course consists of a series of short bulletin inserts
    that will begin to prepare the adult community
    for what lies ahead.
You might also use them as reflection pieces
    for staff meetings, parent meetings,
    or catechist training sessions.
You will also find excellent educational ideas
    in the Leader's Guide for *Our Hearts Were Burning Within Us*.

STEP 3. INVITE FOLKS IN THE PARISH TO BEGIN SHARING THEIR FAITH

If all you do for the entire first year
    of whole community catechesis activities in your parish
    is faith sharing,
        you have done a great deal!
Faith sharing opens the door for folks
    to meet and know and walk with Christ
    in their everyday lives.
It shifts the basis on which parish decisions are made
    from the business of the parish
    to the mission of Christ and the gospel.
If you, as the staff and key volunteers,
    are enthusiastic about sharing faith,
    and if you share yourselves,
    then others in the parish will follow suit.

Once you decide to proceed,
    simply begin using the Question of the Week
    as described in chapter three.
Assign to one of the staff persons
    the job of preparing a weekly faith sharing guide,
    following the sample provided in this handbook.
Use the bulletin short course in chapter seven
    to help the whole community understand
    why and how faith sharing is done.
Help folks see the connection
    between sharing faith
      and catechesis,
    between the Sunday assembly
      and catechesis assemblies,
    between life in their own household
      and catechesis,
    between the pastoral ministries of the parish
      and catechesis.
If possible, begin including the Question
    at the end of each week's homily
    in the Sunday assembly
    to assist the whole community
      in breaking open the Word.

Encourage faith sharing as a staff
    by doing it yourselves.
Use it at every parish meeting,
    choir rehearsal,
    pastoral council meeting,
    faculty meeting,
    and every other opportunity.
Invite folks to use the same method of sharing
    in their homes.
To aid this, print the Question of the Week
    in the Sunday bulletin
    and encourage people to talk about it
    in the car on the way home
      from the Sunday assembly,
    at supper on Sunday evening,
    or whenever they decide is best for them.
If necessary, repeat the bulletin short course
    as an introduction to faith sharing,
    which will help folks understand why and how it's done.

STEP 4. LAUNCH A SERIES OF LIVING WITH CHRIST PARISH RETREATS

to help folks root themselves more deeply
in Christ.
Helping folks develop a lively, animated faith life—
one that includes
personal prayer,
Scripture study,
celebration of the sacraments, especially the Eucharist,
contributions to parish community life,
and a deep desire for justice and peace—
that could sum up the work of the gospel, couldn't it?
Such is the aim of a retreat program
offered within the parish,
a short retreat offered each month
that is designed to fit into people's busy lives
but is packed with the essentials
of what it means to live with Christ.
Once you decide to proceed,
follow the step by step check lists in chapter three
to begin organizing for these retreats.

STEP 5. MAKE AN ANNOUNCEMENT

At some point,
when everything seems ready,
announce that a new day is dawning
in the parish catechetical ministries.
No longer will there be a program
designed solely for children.
Now the program will involve everyone
in the parish,
whether or not there are children
in the household.
Everyone will be invited
to participate in catechesis.
The program will flow
from the readings in the Sunday assembly.
It will develop more meaningful class sessions
and may include some catechesis assemblies
that will be intergenerational,
where whole families can attend together.
Those with the vocation to be a catechist
will assist others in learning more about their faith
and living according to it.

Rather than religious education for children
    culminating in the reception of the sacraments,
    the parish will be undertaking a process
        aimed at young working people,
        senior members of the community,
        those in special circumstances in their lives,
        and yes, the children,
            the teens,
            and persons of every age group.
To everyone's surprise, there will be
    widespread acceptance of this new approach
    and also widespread participation in it.

STEP 6. LAY OUT A SIMPLE PLAN TO IMPLEMENT THIS CHANGE

Again, *Our Hearts Were Burning Within Us* Leader's Guide
    has excellent resources
    to help you write a sound and workable plan.
As you plan and schedule
    the first catechesis assemblies,
    be flexible and seek the input of everyone
        in your leadership circle.
Invite everyone to give feedback
    in those first months,
    and receive the feedback graciously.
Keep your plan simple.
For catechesis assemblies, for example,
    you need only a large room,
    round tables,
    table leaders,
    a lead catechist,
    a well-planned faith sharing and closing liturgy,
    good food,
    and a good microphone.
It really is less complicated
    than organizing
    all those classes and volunteer catechists,
        as you may do in your present system.
Keep talking about this process
    in the new language of whole community catechesis,
    gradually teaching people
        to stop calling it CCD
        or religious ed
        and to start calling it by its new name.

Remember, you are launching a new approach,
>following a framework
>that is new in catechesis for many people.
Do not abandon your present children's programs,
>but allow them to gradually be transformed
>into events that more and more
>>attract and serve the adult community
>>as well as the children.
You will begin to see amazing changes as you proceed.
Catechist knowledge and readiness will improve,
>children will be more engaged in the process,
>more connections will be made to everyday life,
>and more parents will be present for more of the program.

STEP 7. ADJUST YOUR PARISH SCHEDULE AND BUDGETS

Schedule the use of parish meeting rooms and spaces
>to accommodate the catechesis assemblies
>and the Living with Christ retreats.
The parish budget will not have to change very much,
>but there are some important shifts to bear in mind.
Salaries will remain as they are currently
>in your faith formation program budget.
The staff you now have may change job descriptions
>but will still be needed
>to continue organizing meaningful classroom sessions
>or to organize whole community catechesis activities.
But you may need to add the following:
>a stipend for the lead catechists for the large assemblies
>>or for meetings within households;
>the cost of using media of various kinds in the assemblies;
>the cost of the Living with Christ retreats,
>>which is not covered by the fee you charge the participants;
>and the cost of materials printed locally or purchased
>>to provide religious instruction
>>for the adults as well as the children.
The budget for the parish will also slowly become less departmental
>as catechesis, liturgy, and pastoral care
>all begin working more closely together.

STEP 8. DO ALL THIS IN THE CONTEXT OF FAITH SHARING AND PRAYER

Every single day at Vatican II,
    the bishops of the world
    prayed together for the Holy Spirit
    to enter into and lead their discussions
        and decisions.
During certain council sessions
    the crowds out in St. Peter's Square
     chanted *Veni Creator Spiritus*,
        (Come Holy Spirit)
      as the voting proceeded
         inside the basilica.
Throughout the council there was a strong sense
    that the Holy Spirit was in charge,
    guiding and helping.
This shift to whole community catechesis
    comes about under the influence,
       guidance,
       and comfort
    of that very same Spirit.

After all, we aren't pushing our own agenda.
We aren't advancing some sort of political
    or financial campaign.
We know because of our own faith sharing
    that we do this work for one reason only:
    for Christ's sake!
We want to help people meet Christ,
    be converted,
    believe,
    and live by faith, in the Church.
This is the work of Christ in today's world,
    not our own work.
Our ministry calls us to be flexible,
    open,
    generous,
    and charitable
       in our dealings with others.

STEP 9. KEEP COMMUNICATING

This is a huge key to success
> in making the shift to whole community catechesis.

Once people see the new method unfold,
> it doesn't take long for them
> to become participants.

Communication then becomes much easier,
> much more word-of-mouth.

When talking about whole community catechesis in the beginning,
> keep making these main points.

First, catechesis is a lifelong journey of faith
> that moves people ever more deeply
> into the heart of the Lord,
>> through the Church community.

People will gradually make the shift
> from thinking of catechesis as something just for the kids
> to thinking of it as necessary for everyone.

Second, every parish member is part of this.
> Catechesis is done by and for everyone.

It's an activity of the parish and at the same time
> the parish itself is being taught.

Catechesis is not the task of a few staff people
> or a few volunteers
> but of the entire parish community,
> and within it
>> each household in its own way.

Third, to some extent, whole community catechesis
> must *unfold* under the watchful eye of parish leaders.

Patience and trust are needed.
> Not everything can happen at once;
> not all dimensions of parish life can change
>> in the same week!

Parishes need a certain level of stability
> and predictability
> in order to function well.

People coming to the Church, especially at times of great need,
> must know what to expect:
>> at times of death,
>> when there is the loss of love,
>> during oppression or fear
>> when they are suffering illness,
>>> material poverty,
>>> or spiritual hunger.

Fourth, whole community catechesis does call for change
     on two important levels:
     parish and personal.
On the personal level, more people will be called
     to renew their own faith more often.
This will be challenging to many
     but welcomed by most!
On the parish level, changes will occur as well.
     Parish and school religious education schedules
          will be adjusted,
     the use of parish and school space will change,
     and staff job descriptions in the parish or school may change.
Change can be threatening and frightening for people.
     We need to guide the parish carefully
     through this transition.

Here's what one pastor told me about his experience
     as they launched a more complete whole community catechesis process
     in that parish:

At first I was not really in favor of this. I thought it would have a major impact on the whole parish, and I wasn't ready for that. Nevertheless, in one meeting where some other staff members were objecting, saying they felt this was just too much change all at once, I suddenly found myself defending it. The words just came out of my mouth. I told them that this would deepen the average person's grasp of theology, spirituality, and Church life, something that's been declining in our parish. It would increase the number of people who are active in their faith, and some of them will also be active in the parish. It will increase contributions, I told them, because when every household signs on, that's our stewardship campaign right there.

Having these intergenerational assemblies will make the kid's programs more effective, not less, I told them. And it will improve the Sunday assembly because it will unite us. Instead of three or four departments within the parish, we'll operate much more interactively with each other. Pastoral care, for example, flows from liturgy as people share viaticum with the sick. Catechesis improves liturgical practice as folks are more knowledgeable of their faith. Evangelization happens naturally as households take on the task of living a Christian life. We all have the same mission in this parish, after all.

And all of this, I finished, will force us [the staff] to work to a higher standard. We ourselves will return to catechesis if we really believe it's a lifelong process. But also, it will make our work more satisfying. We won't be pulling at straws anymore.

I know this won't be an easy shift. But just think ahead five years: the whole community involved in catechesis, and not just the kids! We have to do this, I told them, because it's the right thing to do.

■ A FOOTNOTE

You may encounter difficulty
    in the process of sharing this with others.
The vision of whole community catechesis
    is somewhat hard to see
    unless the people involved are personally connected
        to Jesus Christ.
This isn't like a business decision
    where the budget must first add up
    or the decision is trounced.
It isn't a personal decision
    in which the parish director or coordinator
    or the school principal
    begins the process on a personal whim.
Whole community catechesis is a matter
    of undertaking the pedagogy of Jesus
    as the GDC describes it in articles 139-140.
In those articles you'll find the following:
    "In [Christ's] words, signs, and works
    during his brief but intense life,
    the disciples had direct experience of the fundamental traits
        of the "pedagogy of Jesus,"
        and recorded them in the gospels:
        receiving others, especially the poor, the little ones and sinners,
            as persons loved and sought out by God;
            the undiluted proclamation of the Kingdom of God
                as the good news of the truth
                and of the consolation of the Father;
            a kind of delicate and strong love
                which liberates from evil and promotes life;
            a pressing invitation to a manner of living
                sustained by faith in God,
                by hope in the kingdom,
                and by charity to one's neighbor;
            the use of all the resources
            of interpersonal communications,
                such as word, silence, metaphor, image, example,
                and many diverse signs
                as was the case with the biblical prophets.
Inviting his disciples to follow him unreservedly and without regret,
    Christ passed on to them his pedagogy of faith
    as a full sharing in his actions and in his destiny."

Now pause here for just one minute
    and go back to reread
    this section of the GDC.
Read it aloud if you can,
    or at least mouth the words silently
    if you can't.
Take the time
    to write this out in your own words,
    phrase by phrase.
        This section is the key,
        the centerpoint of the GDC.
These articles contain a job description for those who would work
    in whole community catechesis.
When you pause to see it,
    it's clear that no one can take on this pedagogy,
    no one can embrace this ministry
        who is not steeped
        in the paschal mystery of Christ.
No one can learn this
    "manner of living sustained
    by faith in God,
    by hope in the kingdom,
    and by charity to one's neighbor"
        without a teacher or catechist.
No one can grow like this
    without being a disciple of someone
    who already has a deep faith.

We live in an exciting time!
We are in the process as a Church community
    of shifting to a catechetical approach
    that will lead many to the heart of Christ.
The·whole community,
    people of all ages,
    will be coming forward seeking formation.
As Maria Harris says in *Fashion Me a People*,
    "It isn't so much that the parish
        has a religious education program—
            that's the language of the past.
But today we would say that the parish
    is a learning community.
The parish is a process of catechesis!
    That's what defines a parish, in part."
Amen.

CHAPTER THREE

Providing Opportunities for Conversion Experiences

Introduction

As we have already seen in earlier parts of this handbook,
a significant aspect of whole community catechesis
is to provide opportunities within the parish
for personal and parish-wide conversion.
This chapter provides the framework
for two such conversion opportunities;
much of this material is in reproducible format.

The first is a parish-based retreat experience
which, when used faithfully,
will utterly change the tenor of your community
almost from the beginning.
Many good things will come from it
for the parish community:
increased stewardship,
increased willingness to serve,
stronger commitment,
a deeper understanding of the faith,
and a desire for instruction.
Many good things will also occur
within people's lives
as they turn their hearts ever more to Christ.

The second is the now-familiar parish-wide faith sharing process
and a guide for launching it within the parish.
Again, parishes that faithfully encourage faith sharing,
where the leaders themselves share faith,
are alive in the Spirit!

m. nakomaki

Why retreats are important for Christians

Throughout the Church's long history
people have always made retreats.
Sometimes the retreat is a silent weekend
with a few presentations
and spiritual direction.
Other times it's a more shared experience,
comparing notes and stories with others.
Sometimes the retreat lasts an entire week
or even a whole month.

Other times it's shorter,
    whether one day
    or several evenings in a row.
Whatever the format,
    content,
    or schedule may be,
    the purpose of the retreat is always the same:
to draw closer to the heart of the Lord,
    to allow Christ to grow within,
    to intentionally open our lives to the action of the Spirit.

The outcome of the retreat is also plain:
    a deeper conversion to Christ
        so as to live with and in Christ more fully
        on a daily basis.
This means bringing into one's own life,
    one's relationships and household,
    the teachings of Jesus of Nazareth:
        forgiveness,
        generosity,
        hospitality,
        love for the materially poor,
        awareness of God's reign,
        and a heart for justice and peace.

Turning to Christ in this way
    is natural for us humans.
It's not so much an ideal outside of ourselves
    as an inner hunger and drive,
    an integral part of who we are
        at our very core.
We have, you might say,
    an inborn hunger for God.

A retreat is a time to allow the divine force
    to well up within us,
    to fill us with love and power,
    to grant us the intuition of presence.
A retreat is, in short,
    a pathway to conversion.

THE FIRST STEP

In whole community catechesis,
 conversion of this sort is the first step.
Good catechesis occurs only when we
 first turn our hearts to Christ,
 first experience conversion,
  and prepare for a lifelong process
  of this turning.
For parents, isn't this important
 if you hope your children
 will follow you in the faith?
Don't you yourselves first need to know Christ
 so that your household
 can be aglow with divine love?
For young adults, isn't this conversion process
 what will lead you to a more mature faith
 as you grow in life experience?
For parish leaders,
 without having Christ at the center
 of all that happens within the community,
  how can you hope for success?
What ministry are you in if not this?
For parish staff,
 isn't it true that repeatedly turning your heart to Christ,
 repeatedly pausing to soak in the divine presence,
  is essential to your ministry?
Aren't you, above all, called to a more profound life in Christ,
 to a daily walk with the Lord?
For senior members of the parish community,
 what better time than now
 to deepen your own faith
  and to invite others to follow you?
For those who are struggling with faith,
 why not pause
 and allow Christ to enter your heart?
  There is no other real source
  of happiness and peace.

Faith sharing, we have said earlier,
 is one key avenue to conversion.
When we share our faith with others,
 even if we are doubtful or unsure,
 our faith somehow becomes more real for ourselves.

When we share our faith,
    we ourselves grow
    and so do those around us.
This sharing, whether with a close friend,
in a circle of companions,
    or in larger groups,
        leads us to discover Christ
        who is already present.
Christ himself lived and worked with his own companions.
    His spiritual life
    was marked by faith sharing.
He shared his own faith in a loving God,
    his own belief in forgiveness,
    his own trust in the divine hand,
    his own need for friendship,
        assurance,
        and a shared life.
Contrary to popular Western belief,
    Jesus was not a loner.
He was not some lonely cowboy-like figure
    who rode the back roads of Galilee
    without need of companions.
Rather, he revealed to us God who is love,
    love in the first person:
        intimacy,
        companionship,
        and community.

The "community of God"
    the Trinity,
    is the clearest revelation
        that we need each other.
We need companions for the journey,
    others whose hearts we know
    and whose voices we trust.

NOT MUCH TIME

At the parish level,
    life moves fast.
The schedules are packed, and there isn't much time
    for things that aren't in that schedule.
Faith sharing is one of the things
    most often put off by parish staff.
"There just isn't time," is the excuse.

But, of course, this undermines
    the very purpose of the parish.
The first and foremost role of the parish
    is to provide a place
    where people can meet Christ
    in the life of the community.
Toward that end,
    parishes provide Sunday assemblies,
        catechesis,
        the catechumenate,
        other sacramental celebrations,
        pastoral care,
        and work for justice and peace.
However, it's possible to so fill parish life
    with activities of these kinds
    that Christ himself is overlooked.
It's possible to be so concerned with "getting it all done"
    that we fail to do the most important thing:
        to be companions to each other,
        to share faith in Christ,
        to grow in God's love,
        and to allow the Spirit room to play.

One excellent way to change that
    is to organize a series of retreats
    held at the parish itself.
The best way toward this end
    seems to be a retreat that is:
        held at times when people are free;
        short enough to be doable;
        long enough to have an effect;
        inexpensive enough not to break the budget;
        simple enough to be run by the parish itself;
        and often enough to provide its benefits
        to many people.
Such a retreat can happen
    with two evenings (Thursday and Friday)
    and one morning (the next day, Saturday).
A once-a-month schedule of these
    provides a steady flow in parish life.
It allows almost 600 people each year
    to deepen their commitment to Christ and the Church.
This schedule enables many others to enter into ministry
    on behalf of those making the retreats.

A PROFOUND EFFECT

Developing a parish level retreat program
    has a profound and dramatic effect
    on the life of the whole community.
Such retreats have a threefold effect.

First, those making the retreat really do experience
    a renewed life in Christ.
They receive the means they need for ongoing conversion
    and the companions they need
    to make that work.
This tends to make them more active in parish life,
    more willing to contribute money for common needs,
    and more effective in their ministry roles.

Second, parish leaders and staff people
    are confronted constantly by this core mission:
    helping folks meet and know Christ.
This core mission is never far from their consciousness:
    it's front and center all the time.
The retreat leads to improved Sunday assemblies,
    a more engaged parish community overall,
    and an excitement and energy
        often lacking, as parishes today
        cope with large work loads and small staffs.

Third, since the first ones we recruit for these retreats
    are the parish leaders themselves,
    the whole tone of the parish shifts gears.
The work of the pastor and staff is made so much easier
    when hundreds of people turn their hearts to Christ
    because spirituality becomes
        the heart of the parish.
This spirituality drives evangelization,
    outreach,
    pastoral care for the sick and imprisoned,
    stewardship,
    work for justice in the neighborhoods,
    and catechesis.

Planning and preparation

Following is a format for just such a parish retreat.
This is a well-tested format,
    easily doable and not expensive.
It's carefully laid out to lead folks
    to be aware of their faith journeys,
    to reconnect with the paschal mystery,
    to pray with the Scriptures again,
    to celebrate the sacraments of the Church,
    to see how living in Christ fits into daily life,
    and then to commit themselves to such a life,
        in the context of the parish itself
        with the tools needed to sustain it.
Read through the notes below.
Then call together a team and get started.
    Don't wait.
    This is an important first step
        in developing whole community catechesis.

■ OVERVIEW

This retreat is designed to be used at the local parish level for people who are age 18 years or older. It is organized by leaders in the parish community and carried out entirely by them. Outlines are provided here for all the talks. The maximum number of new retreatants is about fifty, but the retreat is repeated over and over, allowing as many in the parish to participate as want to. In the best situations, one retreat would be held every month, perhaps the first or second week, on a regular schedule.

It runs for two evenings and one Saturday morning. The evenings are Thursday and Friday, the Saturday is the following day. Keeping these three times as close together as possible is best for the flow of the retreat. It can also be run as an all day Friday and Saturday morning retreat but that will be more difficult for working people.

You might consider providing child care for the period of the retreats to allow young couples or single parents with children to be present.

■ ROOM SET-UP

■ A private conference room is needed with round tables, each seating six retreatants plus one leader. Include a podium, and a small table on which the sacred Scriptures will be placed along with a candle. If the lights in the room are bright overhead lights that cannot be dimmed, then bring in lamps to light the room with a more intimate lighting scheme.

- A private dining room, separated from the conference room. The tables here need not be round.

- The use of the church, or another space prepared for worship.

- The scheduling nightmare: rather than making these retreats fit into the existing parish schedule of weddings and other events, put these into the calendar first and schedule everything else around them. What could be more important than helping folks turn their hearts to Christ? And even if all the other events were done, if this is not done, we may fail in our core mission.

■ STAFF

- Someone must be named the coordinator of these retreats. It could be a staff person or a willing volunteer. It can be anyone who is willing and able.

- A retreat leader for each weekend who will provide some of the reflections (a half hour each) and lead the sharing.

- Other speakers or teachers to offer the reflections if the leader does not.

- Table leaders who will lead all activities at that level; one leader is needed for each small group.

- Hosts who will oversee hospitality, meals, and general set up and clean up; the "host team" will be as large as is needed.

- Prayer leader who will invite prayers and good works from the community to support the work of the retreat.

- Roles for the pastor or other priests, and the liturgical musicians.

■ MATERIALS NEEDED

- a Bible for each participant;
- a common Bible to place centrally in the room;
- a Christ candle to place next to the Scriptures;
- a bowl of water to place centrally in the room, near the candle and Scriptures;
- pads for note taking;
- pens;
- decorations for the meeting and dining rooms to make them welcoming and appealing;
- tent style name plates for each table;
- name tags for everyone, including all the leaders;
- Journey of Faith inventory sheets—reproducible sample included in this book;
- materials to make available for the bazaar on Saturday morning (see below);
- prayer service to accompany Reconciliation Form 2 or 3; reproducible samples included in this handbook;
- food for meals; the meals are an integral part of the retreat experience.

Retreat Schedule

Thursday evening	Event	Location
6:00 PM	Supper (served and cleaned up by host team)	Dining room
	Prayer before eating	
6:45 PM	First session: Introductions	Meeting room
7:45 PM	Break (refreshments served by hosts)	
8:00 PM	Proclamation of the Word	
	Second session: The Journey of Faith	Meeting room
	Large group sharing	
10:00 PM	End for the night; everyone sleeps at their own homes	

Friday evening		
6:00 PM	Supper (served and cleaned up by host team)	Dining room
	Prayer before eating	
	At the tables after eating: brief mystagogia	
6:45 PM	Proclamation of the Word	
	Third session: Dying in Christ	Meeting room
7:45 PM	Break (refreshments served by hosts)	
8:00 PM	Fourth session: Healing in the Community	Meeting room
	The sacrament of reconciliation,	Church
10:00 PM	End for the night; everyone sleeps at their own homes	

Saturday morning		
8:00 AM	Breakfast	Dining room
	Prayer before eating	
	At the tables after eating: brief mystagogia	
8:45 AM	Proclamation of the Word	
	Fifth session: Living with Christ	Meeting room
10:15 AM	Break with substantial snack	Dining room
10:45 AM	Sixth session: A Plan for Daily Life	Meeting room
	A bazaar of activities and materials	
11:30 AM	Closing Eucharistic Liturgy	Church

Preparation Checklist

Six weeks before each retreat

- Announce the retreat in the parish. Scheduling will have to be done far in advance to have the needed spaces and people available.

- In many parishes, these retreats will be needed in a variety of languages. Even though immigrants eventually do speak English, most of the time they pray and live their daily faith in their native tongue. You have permission to translate any part of these notes for use in another language.

- Invite people who want to participate to sign up formally and pay a small fee, about $20.00, to defray the cost. Have a small fund available for those who cannot afford to pay. The rest of the cost can come from parish budgets.

- Give personal invitations to all parish staff, elected leaders, and other leaders in the community. Encourage married couples to attend together. The expectation should be that anyone involved in parish life prepares for leadership by making a Living with Christ retreat.

- Limit the number to about forty-eight, in eight groups of six or so, plus leaders for a total of about sixty.

One month before each retreat

- Recruit a "host team" to help with set up, clean up, and meals—probably about eight people. This team can be given all responsibility for this work.

- Recruit a "retreat leader," someone with experience in leading group process and who has already experienced conversion to Christ.

- Recruit "table leaders" to lead table discussions. If necessary, these can be people making their first Living with Christ retreat.

- Schedule a two room space, one to serve as a dining room, near the kitchen, and the other to serve as the meeting room. Snacks will be set out during most of the retreat as well. These can either be on a table in the meeting room or in the dining room. It's necessary for both of these rooms to be private from other parish events. And it's necessary for the meeting room to be available for the entire three day period because people will be leaving things on the tables, hanging papers in the room, and so forth.

- Also schedule the church if possible for reconciliation on Friday evening and again for the closing Eucharist on Saturday at 11:45 AM. If there are conflicts with weddings or funerals, other rooms can be used for the retreat because of the smaller number of people.

- Schedule the pastor and possibly other priests for the sacrament of reconciliation on Friday evening at 8:30 PM.

- Schedule the pastor or another priest and liturgical musicians for the closing liturgy on Saturday at 11:30 AM to 1:00 PM.

- Plan for a way to invite the whole community to pray and keep vigil during the entire retreat period.

  ● One way would be to distribute vigil candles and prayer cards. Ask people to use them at their table during meals throughout the retreat period.

  ● Another way: invite members of the community to offer up works of justice, mercy, and holiness; communicate this to the retreatants by way of a simple note.

  ● The meals are a key part of the retreat experience. They can be simple but elegant. Encourage the host team to develop menus that are easy to prepare and serve.

One week before the retreat

- Confirm with all parish staff members who will be involved to make sure they know the precise time and place they will be needed.

- Meet with the host team leaders to double check all details and supply lists.

- Shop for the needed supplies.

- Review your list of participants and break them into appropriate groups.

- Take a deep breath and relax. The Holy Spirit will be in charge of what happens.

Guide to the first session: Introductions

Folks arrive and are greeted by the team. They receive a name tag. The first event is supper. Many of these people won't know each other very well; this meal is a way for them to begin to enter into the retreat. After supper, adjourn to the meeting room where everyone goes to their tables. It's probably best to pre-assign table seating so that there is a good mix of gender, age, and backgrounds on each table. If the pastor or other parish staff are making this retreat, they simply take their place at a table like anyone else. Once everyone is settled, you are ready to begin.

The retreat leader welcomes everyone

- Tells a little about him or herself, background in the parish, desire to grow in Christ, love for the Church, family details, hopes for this retreat.

- Explains the schedule a little, but only sketchily. Do not give the details or announce beforehand about sacraments, meals, or the topics of the reflections. Let the retreat unfold for the participants a little at a time to keep them focused on the present moment.

- Gives the community guidelines for this retreat:

  - Be kind to each other at all times.

  - Be honest; everything we share at this retreat is confidential.

  - Work hard at this process of growing closer to Christ.

  - Listen carefully to each other

  - Speak clearly, charitably, and briefly when it's your turn.

  - Be open to the Spirit in our midst.

  - Don't keep the group waiting; be on time.

- Asks each group to quickly (in three minutes, timed by the leader) choose a group name and write it on a name plate for the table.

- Then invites each participant to introduce himself or herself: name, family details, life in the parish, hopes for the retreat.

  - Note: the process for this sharing will be the same one used throughout the retreat. Each group comes to the front, standing (or sitting if they are not able to stand) in a line, across the room in front of the podium. Then, one at a time they do their sharing. When all are finished, the large group applauds and the small group goes back to its table.

  - For this first sharing, the small group should first announce its table name and why it was chosen.

- Asks if there are any questions at this point and when all are satisfied, announces the break, asking people to return punctually in fifteen minutes.

Guide to placing the Scriptures, candle, and holy water in the center of the meeting room

After the break

Hold a brief ceremony honoring the Word of God. Process with the Bible to the center of the room, holding the Bible reverently above your head and place it on the table. Light the candle. Proclaim a short reading. Then say that the Bible is the light for our lives and the life of the whole Church. It will also be the center of what we do here in the next three days. Give a very short explanation of why this is so. Then reflect that baptism is the beginning of our journey of faith. At baptism we receive Christ, we are empowered by grace to live in Christ. The water of baptism is a sign of this new life. Then sprinkle all with this water as an opening blessing. This entire opening ceremony should take ten minutes or less.

Guide to the second session:
Talk outline for The Journey of Faith

This is a fifteen-minute reflection given by either the retreat leader or someone else chosen for this presentation, the purpose of which is to help the participants become aware that growing in faith is a lifelong journey begun at baptism and continuing down through the years. It is intentional, basic, and something we share in the parish community.

- Thank you for being here this week.

- Our spiritual journey, I suppose you could say, started at baptism for us.

- But many came before us, parents, grandparents, neighbors, all the way back to the time of Christ and beyond.

- Down through history, a parade of faithful people have come to know Christ, to turn their hearts to Christ, and to live according to the teachings of Christ as presented by the Church.

- So with us. Pause for a moment, think back over your own journey:

  - Remember religious ed?

  - What religion did you practice as a child?

  - What do you remember about those years in your faith life?

  - What was happening in your family or in the world that affected your faith journey?

  - What were some turning points in your life?

  - What brought you here tonight?

- Taking the time to think about our journey helps us steer a clear path toward Christ. We're all so busy all the time. We run from this to that. We come running into church on Sundays, and then run out and keep the race going. Pausing to savor Christ's love, to become more aware of Christ around us, and to share that with each other is what this retreat is about.

- Distribute a Journey of Faith inventory (see page 72), and ask people to take a few minutes to think through it. Then lead each small group to share, giving each person about three minutes (twenty minutes overall).

- Then lead a large group discussion as above, each small group member is invited to share (briefly) with the whole group about one major turning point in his or her spiritual journey.

- When this is finished, go immediately to the closing prayer of the night, which is called "compline." (Compline is an ancient form of liturgical prayer in the Church. It is traditionally prayed to honor the end of the day.)

Guide to the brief ceremony of compline before people go home

- Turn down the lights in the room.

- Have a charcoal lit for incense. Use the Scripture and candle table for this. Check beforehand to see if anyone in the room will have difficulty breathing if incense is used and always use it in moderation in any case. Be sure the room is well ventilated.

- Begin with a sacred gesture: the Sign of the Cross.

- Invite everyone to pause in gratitude for all that has happened this day.

  ● Invite everyone to forgive those who have hurt them and to be sorry for those whom they have hurt.

- Proclaim a short reading from the Word of God: Luke 2:29–32

- Sprinkle a little incense on the charcoal and invite everyone to be silent for a few minutes.

- After two minutes of silence, play a quiet spiritual song on a CD player.

- During the music, pray a simple prayer to end the day.

  Lord, you have given us the generous gift of this day. Now as we prepare to sleep, gently hold our hearts in your hands. Bring us safely through the night to tomorrow, when we will rise to serve you once again. Amen.

- Let the music stop. Blow out the candle. Depart quietly.

Guide to the supper mystagogia on Friday evening and Saturday morning at breakfast

■ After the meal is eaten, but while everyone is still at table, get the attention of the group. Recall the work of the last evening, listing from beginning to end: the opening prayer at supper, the menu, the introductions, spiritual journey talk, sharing, compline.

■ Ask at random (not everyone needs to share):

● What touched you last night?

● What moment still has your attention?

● What's hanging around inside your own heart about what we did?

■ Allow about five or ten minutes for this sharing and then dismiss the group to return to the meeting room.

■ The mood of this should be light. Humor and anecdote are welcome.

Guide to the third session:
Talk outline for Dying in Christ

This is a fifteen-minute reflection given either by the retreat leader or by someone else chosen for this presentation, the purpose of which is to help participants see that in order for us to live in the light of Christ, we need to experience the paschal mystery: we must die to ourselves in Christ (the first must be last, the most important must be the servant of all), and be aware of our shortcomings so the grace of Christ can truly transform our lives. We need to distinguish between "unhealthy" dying, which implies allowing oneself to be enslaved by ideology or stronger persons, and "healthy" dying, which is always motivated by a deep love for others and oneself.

- Throughout the journey of faith in our lives, we have opportunities to either live as Christ teaches or to turn to another teacher, whatever or whoever that might be.

- Proclaim Luke 6:17–38. When you are finished, ask the participants to open their own Bibles to review it. It's the sermon on the plain. Here is a good summary of Jesus' teachings. (Go through them together, commenting, giving examples, inviting participants to mark up the text or take notes on their notepads.) Use other biblical phrases to show the pattern in the text of asking us to die to ourselves and live in Christ.

- When we don't measure up, or when we miss the mark, it's time to pause and see what happened. Why didn't we love our enemies? Why did we keep gossiping? Why did we cling to money? Why did we ignore the materially poor, especially when there was so much we could have done? (Continue with a short examination of conscience.)

- At these times we have to admit that we let someone else be our leader and teacher: the group we hang with, our families, our society, our government or president, the promise of comfort from money, and so on.

- Now pause and ask yourself, how have I failed to live up to the teachings of Christ? How do I need to die to myself in order to know the joy of living with Christ?

- Invite a small group sharing again, then the same format for large group sharing as the previous evening. In the large group, ask each participant to share (briefly) one way they could do better at dying in Christ.

- After the sharing is complete, announce a break.

Guide to the fourth session:
Talk outline for Healing in the Community

This is a fifteen-minute reflection given by the leader or someone else, the purpose of which is to help the participants see that the Church offers ways for them to experience the healing power of Christ. One of these is the sacrament of reconciliation.

- In the old days, to some people confession meant simply listing sins and telling them to the priest who then prayed over us, gave us a penance, and sent us home to "sin no more."

- But of course, we did sin again, didn't we?

- Today the focus of this sacrament is on healing. It's on the unending mercy of God. We prepare and come to the priest to talk about trends in our lives, ways in which we are moving away from the heart of the Lord. Of course, we must also still be sorry for our sins and willing to accept God's mercy, extended to us through the sacrament of the Church. Examples:

  - I'm just so wrapped up in materialism.

  - I find it so hard to help the materially poor by giving them my money.

  - Sometimes I feel just so selfish.

  - I really haven't been praying much lately.

  - There is just a lot of anger within me and I don't know why.

- The Church invites us to consider not only the personal aspect of being off the mark, of sinning, but also the social aspects of living that way.

- Through the sacrament of reconciliation, we make our return to the Lord. We get back on the path of our spiritual journey of faith.

- Tonight we offer you this chance. If you don't wish to celebrate the sacrament, you may spend this time in quiet with the rest of the group. (Now go with the group to the church, moving quietly.)

  - To help people prepare for this sacrament, have cards with the format of the sacrament available. Many will not recall the last time they celebrated it. Also, to help them prepare, provide a short examination of conscience.

  - Use the outline on pages 73-74 as a guide for celebrating the sacrament.

  - End the celebration with a closing prayer service.

After the celebration of the sacrament

Hold a brief closing party with wine and cheese and music back in the dining room. All can join in this party, including the priests, musicians, and others.

Guide to the fifth session:
Talk outline for Living with Christ

This is a fifteen-minute reflection given by the leader or someone else chosen for this job, the purpose of which is to help the participants see how their journey now continues into their everyday lives. They will be asked to identify what will help them live with Christ more closely day by day.

- The gospels show how the journey of faith is lived. We come to know Christ and to die to ourselves in loving others, as Christ did for us. This leads us to a rhythm in our lives of pausing, examining our consciences, celebrating God's mercy, and moving on. (Share your own personal story of this.)

- Proclaim a reading from the Word of God: Romans 12:1–2.

- We are called into service. God's presence in our lives is always giving us a nudge toward love, always toward love. To help the materially poor by ending the causes of poverty. To visit the imprisoned. To care for an aging parent or friend. To bring viaticum, oil, and friendship to the ill. To care for a sick friend. To speak on behalf of the voiceless, the rejected, and the marginalized of our culture. People are called in many ways. Each call is unique but all of them taken together show how God is caring for the world.

- One thing about this: the call is more than merely making money, or getting famous, or being comfortable, or being "right" about your theology or politics. The call is to serve:

  ● To what or to whom are you called?

- Each person on this journey of faith needs different tools. For some it's a small group with which to share Scripture and faith sharing. For others, it's a monthly gathering like this, to help keep them on track. For still others, it's a prayer guide, helping them know and love the Scriptures.

  ● What will help you answer God's call in your life?

- Small group sharing, followed by large group sharing as above. (To whom are you called? What tools will you need?)

- After the sharing announce a break. This break will have more substantiaL food in it because there really is no lunch being served.

Guide to the sixth session:
Talk outline for A Plan for Daily Life with Christ

This is a fifteen-minute reflection given by the leader or someone else designated for this job, the purpose of which is to assist participants in formulating a concrete plan that will help them continue to live with Christ after the retreat. The hosts will set up an exhibit-like event in the dining room which participants will roam through and learn or sign up or purchase. This will help folks get involved in the parish community, or wider community. Time and talent sign up can happen here, stewardship commitments can be made here. Items can be for sale.

- All the good intentions in the world don't help when you are back in the routine of your daily life. What we need then is a plan.

- Like those in AA, if we don't have a plan to continue the journey, we will soon find we're off the path.

- Give an example of this from your own life.

- Stress the importance of a daily life style that supports the Christian journey:
  - household meals
  - regular prayer
  - being part of a community
  - being in the Sunday assembly
  - sharing faith with others

- After the reflection, before you dismiss them to browse through the offerings in the dining room, show them several good items from the podium. Show them how to get involved, how to organize their lives for prayer, and so forth.

- After about twenty minutes of browsing, gather everyone back to prepare for the Eucharist.

Guide to the closing Liturgy of the Word and Eucharist

■ Where permitted, this can be the weekend liturgy.

■ This should be a more intimate liturgy than usual. Try to use a small space in an intimate setting.

■ Music should be kept simple and singable.

■ Invite the retreatants to take appropriate roles in the Mass as readers, eucharistic ministers, and so forth.

■ After the homily, pause and invite the participants who wish to do so, to share briefly about their experience on this retreat. Similar to the mystagogia at the meals, walk back through the events of the three days and recount them briefly. Then ask what has touched them. What has impressed them or opened new insights?

■ Choose a Eucharist Prayer appropriate to this group.

■ After the communion rite, the presider might consider giving a special blessing to send them on their way.

Journey of Faith Inventory

The purpose of this brief reflection tool is to help you focus on your own journey of faith in your life so far. Please pause quietly for a few minutes to respond to the questions. Then, if you are comfortable doing so, prepare to share with others whatever part you wish.

When and where, as much as you can remember...

1. My baptism

Who decided you should be baptized?

2. The household I was raised in

Who was part of that household?

How much was religion practiced there?

Describe the spirituality of your household

prayerful?

justice centered?

non-existent?

pious?

progressive or conservative?

more than one religious background?

3. My early parish experiences

Name and location of parish?

How were you involved?

Thinking back, what do you remember most?

4. How I responded to religion during young adulthood

As you entered college or the work force, what role did religion play in your life?

Who were your most influential friends, teachers, or ideas?

5. Turning points in my adult life regarding my faith

Influential people

Influential ideas

Influential life events

6. My current connection to religion and a parish

Name and location of parish?

How are you or aren't you involved?

What attracts or repels you in parish life?

7. My current connection to Christ and the spiritual life

Describe your own current prayer life

Where do you find inspiration and guidance for life?

The Sacrament of Reconciliation Prayer Service

For use in the context of a Living with Christ retreat during which the penitents will have already examined their consciences.

LEADER   (using these or similar words)
> Please pause for a moment,
>> to collect the events of today
>>> and bring ourselves, body and soul,
>>>> into this gathering.

A moment of sacred silence.

LEADER   (using these or similar words)
> Friends, we now gather here as God's family,
> baptized as we are into Christ
>> and walking with Christ
>> on our journey of faith.
> May we celebrate this sacrament of reconciliation
>> conscious of God's mercy
>> and open to God's voice within and among us.

ALL
> In the name of God. Amen.

LEADER
Invite all to listen to, sing or recite the opening song-prayer

Reading from Sacred Scripture

READER   *A reading from the letter of Paul to the Ephesians (Eph 4:23–32)*

You were taught to put away your former way of life, your old self, corrupt and deluded by its lusts, and to be renewed in the spirit of your minds, and to clothe yourselves with the new self, created according to the likeness of God in true righteousness and holiness.

So then, putting away falsehood, let all of us speak the truth to our neighbors, for we are members of one another. Be angry but do not sin; do not let the sun go down on your anger, and do not make room for the devil. Thieves must give up stealing; rather let them labor and work honestly with their own hands, so as to have something to share with the needy. Let no evil talk come out of your mouths, but only what is useful for building up, as there is need, so that your words may give grace to those who hear. And do not grieve the Holy Spirit of God, with which you were marked with a seal for the day of redemption. Put away from you all bitterness and wrath and anger and wrangling and slander, together with all malice, and be kind to one another, tenderhearted, forgiving one another, as God in Christ has forgiven you.

The word of the Lord

ALL

Thanks be to God for these words of Scripture!

Confession of Sins

Using the rites of reconciliation, proceed with the general confession and absolution, using the formmost appropriate for your group.

Concluding Prayer of the Church

LEADER   O God, you have called us to baptism in Christ.

ALL   We embrace our baptism with faith.

LEADER   And in that calling you promise us your unending mercy.

ALL   We accept your mercy with thanksgiving.

LEADER   We now stand before you ready to receive forgiveness and in need of your wisdom, strength, courage, and love.

ALL   O God, give us your love.

LEADER   May the Church prepare the world to see you.

ALL   And may the world respond in faith.

LEADER   And for each other here we pray that we might be earnest in our search for truth and fair in our judgments of others.

ALL   May we seek the truth and be fair in all we do and say.
          Amen. Amen. Amen.

Blessing

LEADER   May God who loves us deeply

ALL   O God, we love you without end.

LEADER   May the Spirit who is our Guide

ALL   O Spirit, we listen to your voice.

LEADER   And may Jesus Christ in whose name we gather

ALL   O Jesus, we adore you.

LEADER   Now bless us, direct us, and be with us in love, now and forever.

ALL   We receive your blessing with full hearts.
          Amen. Amen. Amen.

Faith Sharing: a form of adult catechesis

"The baptismal catechumenate," Chris Weber has said,
    "is first and foremost about bringing participants
    into relationship with Jesus Christ
        and helping them turn to him
        with their whole hearts.
Is this task the first priority of the catechetical programs
    in our parish or school?"
        (NCCL *Catechetical Leadership*, volume 12, no. 2)

Baptism is no guarantee

Unfortunately, baptism is no guarantee of conversion.
For some, the faith begins with great vigor,
    but they lose heart after a while.
For others, their faith was never deep
        but remained on the surface of their lives
        until something better or more interesting
            came along.
And for still others, perhaps many others,
        baptism was just not taken very seriously
            to begin with!
Perhaps they were baptized as an infant
        but raised in a home where faith
        is not part of everyday life.
Consequently, these have never come to know Christ
        as part and parcel of their everyday lives.

Jesus spoke of faith like this in the gospel.
The writers of the *General Directory* saw in this
        the seeds for everything they wrote
        about the renewal of catechesis in our day and age:
"A sower went out to sow.
        And as he sowed, some seed fell on the path,
        and the birds came and ate it up.
Other seed fell on rocky ground,
        where it did not have much soil,
        and it sprang up quickly, since it had no depth of soil.
            And when the sun rose, it was scorched;
            and since it had no root,
                it withered away.
Other seed fell among thorns,
        and the thorns grew up and choked it,

and it yielded no grain.
Other seed fell into good soil
    and brought forth grain,
        growing up and increasing
        and yielding thirty and sixty and a hundredfold.
Let anyone with ears to hear listen!" (Mk 4:3–8)

Because the seed of faith is vulnerable
    to the changing soil of one's life
    (to borrow Jesus' metaphor a moment)
        the Church takes great care
        to provide ongoing catechesis
        to nourish faith and help it blossom.
The catechesis which follows upon conversion
    requires a kind of *apprenticeship*.
A catechist takes as apprentices
    others who wish to know
    how to follow the Way of Christ.
It's far more than merely teaching a lesson in a textbook,
    isn't it?
For those in the catechetical process are
    far more than mere students, aren't they?
We can easily see how conversion must be
    the starting element!
Of course, textbook learning has a place
    in helping people
    understand religion and become solid Christians.
The bishops of the Church rightly expect us
    to provide a comprehensive instruction in the faith
        at every level of catechesis.
But the textbook part must come *after* conversion,
when one's heart is in accord with the gospel,
    when it has a chance of making a difference.

Conversion, anyone?

What is the best way to lead someone else
    to turn his or her heart to Christ?
How do you help others experience
    ongoing Christian conversion?
Well, first of all, conversion isn't just for kids!
    Conversion is, in fact,
    really more of an adult experience.

Young people experience an initial conversion,
  learning to love Jesus
  and to desire to be in God's family.
As they grow, they begin to understand
  how this faith influences their way of living.
By being open to the gift of faith,
  the Holy Spirit moves in them
  and creates a desire for prayer,
    for closeness with God,
      and for love of their families and friends.
This keeps happening, in little bits and pieces,
  over and over again,
  poco y poco,
  as they grow in age and grace.

How does conversion happen?

Conversion normally occurs in a communal setting.
  It involves people gathering with others
  in order to share the journey to the heart of the Lord.
    It's a process.
It can't be scheduled in the curriculum.
It doesn't necessarily follow chapter 3, for example,
  in an orderly fashion!
Does this sound a little like the catechumenate?
  Indeed!
  Our understanding of conversion
    flows directly from the spirituality of the RCIA.
In this process, each person looks at the events and people
  of his or her life
  and sees them anew as part of his or her faith.
One then begins to see (slowly at first)
  that one must *die* to oneself
  in order to *rise* with happiness,
  and then *go forth* to love as a follower of Christ.
Conversion of this sort is ongoing throughout life:
  conversion moment followed by conversion moment.
Normally, conversion is a shared experience.
When we stand shoulder-to-shoulder with others
  who are immersed in faith,
  we catch conversion
    and incorporate it into our own lives.
And finally, for almost all Catholics,
  it's also a sacramental experience.

We come to terms with how we must die in Christ
    through baptism and reconciliation.
We find within ourselves a profound desire
    for communion with Christ and our mates.
We experience healing and peace.
And we experience the same excitement
    that those first apostles must have felt
    as we go forth now,
    confirmed in the faith,
        eager to tell others the good news!

For Christ's sake!

All of this is done for Christ's sake,
    not our own.
It is Christ who acts within us when we open ourselves
    to the mystery of faith.
        The opening is the key.
It occurs as described just above
    and, again, it *precedes* catechesis.
In other words, only when we have truly met Christ
    on a deeply personal level,
    and allowed ourselves to enter into Christ's death and resurrection,
    can we begin to understand our faith.
Faith remains a mystery,
    but understanding slowly dawns on us.
In those sacramental moments,
    it is Christ who is the host,
    Christ who sets the table,
    and Christ who acts.
The minister there involved in the leadership represents Christ.

In whole community catechesis,
    people find moments of conversion
    over and over again
        as they break open the Word
        from the Sunday assembly.
Here is a guide to help you get started.

Guide for Parish-wide Faith Sharing

A. DEVELOP A "QUESTION OF THE WEEK" DRAWN FROM THE SUNDAY READINGS.

■ It should be a question that leads to theological reflection without being too theological itself; not a "yes" or "no" question, but one that draws the user deeper into the gospel.

■ A question that asks for a personal response. We aren't looking for a discussion of the faith but a sharing of faith and belief.

■ State the question in plain English, and also offer it in children's terms.

B. WITHIN THE PARISH, THE HOMILIST DELIVERS THIS QUESTION EACH WEEK BY FOCUSING ON IT IN THE HOMILY.

■ If possible, the homilist uses this Question as the final thought in his or her homily. Homilists can thus present the Question to their communities and also share their own faith as a model for others.

■ Repeat the Question of the Week in the bulletin, or in a bulletin insert. Also repeat it in school bulletins, meeting agendas, and other communication tools in the parish.

C. AT PARISH GATHERINGS USE THE QUESTION AS THE OPENING PRAYER IN PLACE OF PRAYER SERVICES.

■ Ask each group that meets to share about this question as the opening prayer of its meeting: staff, councils, committees, ministry groups, the choir, and all others.

■ Provide a brief, one-page Faith Sharing Guide to help people in the parish lead prayer using this formula. A sample of such a guide is provided on the next page. After the proclamation of the Word, pause to allow time for sharing.

■ After the sharing, follow this four-step prayer formula:

● Invite everyone to pause and prepare for prayer.

● Reread part or all of the Sunday gospel or another reading.

● Allow about fifteen minutes for faith sharing based on the Question of the Week. For larger groups, ask the members to split into small groups for the sharing to keep it within fifteen minutes.

● Close with a brief prayer.

D. INVITE MEMBERS OF PARISH HOUSEHOLDS TO SHARE IN THIS SAME WAY.

■ It's naturally ecumenical, inclusive, and catechetical!

■ It helps build the faith life of the household.

Faith Sharing Guide for St. Somebody's Parish

The Call to Prayer

LEADER

My friends, let's pause a moment here in the midst of all our activity to prepare for a few moments of prayer with God and each other.

The Word of God

LEADER   The Lord be with you.

ALL   And also with you.

LEADER   +A reading from the holy Gospel according to _____.

ALL   Glory to you, O Lord.

The gospel reading or a part thereof.

LEADER   This is the gospel of the Lord

ALL   Praise and glory to you, Lord Jesus Christ!

The Faith Sharing

LEADER   This week the parish is sharing faith based on this question:

Present the Question of the Week and allow time for sharing; at the end of the sharing period, invite participants to pray in one of the following ways:

> The Lord's Prayer out loud together
>
> Spontaneous prayers
>
> A moment of silent prayer
>
> Listen to a recorded hymn.

Faith Sharing in Classroom Settings

A. DEVELOP A CHILDREN'S "QUESTION OF THE WEEK" DRAWN FROM THE SUNDAY READINGS

- It should be a question that leads to theological reflection without being too theological itself. Not a "yes" or "no" question, but one that draws the user deeper into the gospel.
- A question that asks for a personal response. We're not looking for a discussion about the faith but a sharing of faith and belief.
- A question that is age appropriate but is still substantial.

B. WITHIN THE SCHOOL OR PARISH RELIGIOUS EDUCATION SESSION, SOMEONE DELIVERS THIS QUESTION EACH WEEK BY SHARING ABOUT IT AS PART OF A PRAYER SERVICE.

- This requires that a special prayer service be held each week, either as an assembly or in each religion session. For Catholic school religion classes, Monday morning is best! By doing this, you teach the young how important it is to share faith.
- Base the prayer service on the readings for either the previous or the upcoming Sunday. Let the gospel reading shape the Question of the Week.
- In the school classrooms you might follow this schedule:

  ● Monday: Hold the school assembly for prayer.

  ● Tuesday: Reread the gospel at the start of the day; ask each student to share faith in a small group setting based on the Question. Invite two or three students to share with the large group. Rotate until everyone has shared with the large group, and then start over!

  ● Wednesday: Reread the gospel again! Invite the students to decide on one way this gospel invites them to change how they live. Work in small groups for this. Ask each small group to "report" to the large group. You might ask them to illustrate their discussion somehow.

  ● Thursday: Reread the gospel yet again! Ask students to work in small groups to compose a prayer based on this gospel reading.

  ● Friday: Hold a classroom prayer service in which the prayers of the students form the basis of the prayer.

- In religious education settings, reread the gospel at the start of the session. Divide the children into small groups and invite them to share their response to the Question of the Week. After a few minutes, invite two or three children to share the insights of their small group with the whole class. Each week, invite a new group to share with the whole class so that all will eventually participate.

C. REPEAT THE QUESTION OF THE WEEK IN THE FAMILY OR SCHOOL BULLETIN, SEND IT HOME, USE IT IN THE FACULTY MEETING AND IN EVERY CLASS OR RELIGION SESSION.

CHAPTER FOUR

A Whole Community Scope and Sequence

Introduction

The *Constitution on Divine Revelation*
    from Vatican II
      helps us understand the relationship
        between Sacred Scripture
        and Sacred Tradition.
We rely on both of them—
    Scripture and Tradition—
    to understand our faith.
It's worth our time here to consider this a little further.

In article three, the *Constitution* says this:
    "In revealing God's inner self,
      God does not merely reveal information
        about the divine life
        but invites us into close companionship.
God actually shares with us the divine nature
    so that we are no longer strangers to God
      or to one another.

God shows us what God is really like,
    and in this process we come to know God's heart
      as God knows ours.
This activity of God revealing God's self to us
    occurs with both words and deeds
    which have an inner unity.
      The deeds of God in history
      confirm the teaching signified by the words
      while at the same time the words
        proclaim the deeds
        and interpret them for us!"
    (taken from *Vatican II in Plain English*)

And in article nine, it concludes this:
"There is a very close connection
    between Scripture on one hand
    and Church Tradition on the other.
They both flow from the same well
    and tend toward the same goal.
Scripture is that written component of the Word of God
    of which we have two volumes:
    Old Testament and New Testament.

Sacred Tradition is the Word of God
     passed on to us in a variety of forms:
          liturgy,
          prayers,
          teachings of the apostles,
          and truths not fully explained in Scripture
               but equally important.
We, therefore, honor both sources of knowledge:
     sacred Scripture and sacred Tradition.
Both Scripture and Tradition are essential components
     of the Word of God."

The *General Directory for Catechesis* also guides us here.
"In much catechesis,
     indeed, reference to sacred Scripture
     is virtually exclusive
     and unaccompanied by sufficient reference
          to the Church's long experience and reflection"
          contained in Church Tradition.
The use of a comprehensive textbook
     bridges this gap
It allows us to combine Scripture and Tradition
     into one source of the faith.
All of us need
     to consider the truths of the faith
     over and over again.
For one thing,
     every time we review them
     the Holy Spirit gives us deeper insight into them.
For another,
     we are able to understand our faith only slowly,
     a little here and a little there.
When we are children in the primary grades, for example,
     only a simple explanation of the Eucharist is possible.
We simply don't possess the life experience
     to understand any more fully.
But as we grow older,
     we understand more.

In the middle grades, we must return to Eucharist,
     we consider other aspects,
     we become familiar with the Body of Christ
          as it lives and breathes around us,
          and we grow more mature in the faith.

By the time we're adults,
 it's time to return again to Eucharist.
I've been in some form of religious education
 for nearly five decades now.
Yet, whenever I read again
  or share faith again
  about the Eucharist,
  I am awed to find yet another key,
  another insight into that wonderful mystery.
So it is throughout life.
Only a comprehensive text
 can provide the insights we need
 to learn about our faith
  and meet Christ.

However, using a textbook also creates a danger.
We do not want to proceed
 without a lectionary connection of some kind.
We do not rely solely on Tradition
 but need to draw firsthand
 from sacred Scripture as well.
Again, throughout life
 we will find that not everything demanded of us
 by the Scriptures
 will be revealed to us on our first reading.
It really is necessary to take the Scriptures with us
 on a lifelong journey of faith.

An outline

The outline you will want to develop
 for instruction in the faith
 for all the members of your community
  is called a scope and sequence.
A scope and sequence is the organized framework,
 the system of lessons and themes
 we follow to present the teachings of the faith
  to a learner.
This framework follows a certain sequence of ideas,
 one after the other.
It stays within a certain scope of topics and themes.
By providing this order,
 a learner has a better chance of getting it all right!

A spiral scope and sequence
    is one in which the learner
    returns to each topic every year
        in spiral fashion.
Each time, the topics are presented
        using age appropriate language
            and teaching methods.

By using a spiral,
    all the students in a single parish or school
        (or both!)
can be studying the same theme at the same time,
        making teacher preparation,
        parental involvement,
        intergenerational groupings,
        and cross cultural teaching
            all much more possible.
In whole community catechesis,
    parishes plan for the involvement
    of the entire community,
        based on this spiral scope and sequence.
Such a plan doesn't mean merely
    that parents are present
    when their children are formed in the faith.
Much more radically, households
    are being formed as Christian homes,
    which involves adult formation for all in the parish.
How on earth will we do that?

First and foremost, parishes will need a religion text
    designed for this purpose.
The whole community
    should study the same themes at the same time.
As I said above,
    a spiral scope and sequence will provide
    themes that both make sense
        and are understandable to people.
Filling people's heads with a lot of doctrine
    doesn't do much good
    unless the presentation is well organized and written.

Your textbook program
    will be the basis of everything else you do.
Think of it this way.

While the first graders
> in both the school and parish programs
> are studying about creation,
>> so are the fifth graders
>> and the teens.
> Extend that study across the parish
> and have material also available
>> for young married couples,
>> middle-aged adults,
>> and senior members of the parish.

Now you truly have the whole community
> working together at catechesis.

Just think how much more powerful that will be!

Outside the elementary program,
> look for materials that will allow you
> to extend your children's catechesis
>> to the rest of the community.

Combine that with faith sharing
> which brings Christ alive in people's hearts,
> and you have a fantastic whole community experience!

The development of a scope and sequence
> for your entire parish community
> is an important first step.

You probably already have the beginnings of what you will need
> in the textbook series
> used in the children's program.

By laying out a plan for all ages at once,
> you can be sure that nothing important
>> is missed
>> or covered too often.

You can organize the material in meaningful ways
> and help persons of all ages
> follow a course of study.

For help in developing this,
> See *Heritage of Faith* by Jo Rotunno.

It provides the groundwork
> you need to proceed.

Begin by sharing your scope and sequence,
> and make it widely visible within the parish.

You might want to create a huge wall display,
> showing each segment of the scope and sequence
> from preschool through senior adult.

Or you may wish to create a "take home" version of it.
Again, you may find another creative way
    to make this tool visible within the parish.

The next step is to begin providing
    both instruction
    and formation.
Instruction will most likely be provided
    using some form of printed materials
    combined with small group discussions
        at times when folks can gather.
We need to be extremely flexible
    and allow this to unfold at its own pace.
We simply cannot organize parishes
    into little theology schools
    where everyone willingly shows up
        when the staff wants them to!
Again, the Leader's Guide for
    Our Hearts Were Burning Within Us
    is loaded with powerful suggestions
        and planning tools to help you do this.

In the end it comes down to providing what people want,
    in the format that best suits them,
    at the times they are most available.
The most immediate contact with adults
    is through the Sunday assembly.
You might work with the liturgical ministers in your parish
    to see how the liturgy can become a vehicle
        for more catechesis.
You might be able to distribute
    some kind of catechetical material
    in connection with the bulletin
        provided it is *short*
        and in *plain English!*
We must avoid too much Church jargon,
    terms that many people don't understand
    or have to work hard to read.
Adults in the Church consistently report
    that if we want the material to hold their interest,
    they must be able to
    understand what they're reading
    and connect it to their everyday life.

Whatever you distribute should have a certain quality of appearance.
Remember that we're competing for people's attention
  with *USA Today*,
  Time magazine,
  and the Internet,
    which are all in color.
I don't mean to offend anyone by saying this,
  but most church bulletins are ugly.
They're printed on poor quality paper
  with odd colored inks,
  and are loaded with advertising,
    which seems to be a big part of the bulletin.
However, with the technology we have today,
  there is no reason to continue with the present format.
The bulletin should be eye-catching,
  full of powerful human stories,
  a public forum for faith sharing,
  a bulletin board for many kinds of announcements,
  and a dynamic tool for adult formation.
Use some of the powerful new software now available
  to design and format what you distribute,
  or purchase a product that is already designed for you
    by one of the publishers.

Don't pass up any opportunity to make available
  materials that are people-friendly,
  and delivered at the appropriate moment.
Use parish meetings,
  special classes,
  Internet chat rooms,
  or any other means you can.
Think of the whole community scope and sequence
  as the framework or agenda
  for this instruction in the faith.
Follow a regular and consistent method
  of providing a systematic and comprehensive
    presentation of the faith.

CHAPTER FIVE

Catechetical Gatherings

We gather

Throughout the Church,
  in all parts of the world,
    people gather or assemble for the purpose
      of sharing catechesis.
Some of these gatherings take place
  under cover of darkness
  for fear of the local authorities.
Some take place in houses made of cane and corn stalks,
  with a tin roof and dirt floor.
Others take place in people's homes,
  parents, children, neighbors,
  small communities of people,
    bound by their faith,
    gathering faithfully together.
And still others take place at parish facilities,
  students meeting in classrooms or assembly halls,
    catechists in place,
    and religion texts in hand.
In this chapter,
  we're going to consider two of these gatherings,
  the classroom and the assembly,
  and provide some ideas about
    how they can catechize the participants
    most effectively.
Reflections on those gatherings in people's homes
  are provided in chapter six
  in our discussion of the domestic Church.

Why not have sponsors?

But before we discuss the various options
  for these gatherings,
  let's consider one other possible tool
    to help learners really grow in their faith
    while helping the whole community participate.
What if every learner
  of any age
  in any catechetical program
    had a sponsor, as they would in the catechumenate?
No one could imagine the catechumenate proceeding
  without a one-on-one sponsor
  for every candidate or catechumen.

Imagine the power of a program of catechesis in a parish
    where each child,
    each young adult,
    or each adult who is enrolled
        also has someone as a mentor!
Here's how this could work.

First, for children and youth,
    why not ask their parents to sponsor them?
After all, it is the role of parents
    to introduce their children to the faith,
        guide them as they grow,
        and witness to them about their own faith.
In cases where one or both parents could not possibly do this,
    either because they do not practice their faith,
    or because of death, separation, divorce, or unwillingness,
        maybe a grandparent would step forward,
        or a godparent,
        or a family friend,
        or a willing member of the parish.
For other possible mentors, call on Catholic friends,
    on neighbors,
    or on willing parish members
        to serve as sponsors.
Mentoring is an element of the catechumenate
    that is ancient and full of wisdom.

Second, the sponsors would be willing
    to attend the catechesis assemblies
    and work with the learners as guide and friend,
        as well as parent or godparent.

Third, the sponsors would be called
    to live a deeply committed Christian lifestyle
    and share their faith with the learners in their care.
Each sponsor's own experience of being Christian,
    of knowing Christ,
    would become a major force in catechesis.

Fourth, then, each sponsor would witness
    to the learner, in age-appropriate words
    about his or her own faith
        as well as the Church's teachings,
        traditions, and rites.

Fifth, each sponsor would be asked to pray daily
     for each learner,
     bringing to mind the learner's particular journey of faith
     and holding the learner to heart.
Sixth, the sponsors would be asked to be with the learners
     in the Sunday assembly whenever possible,
     to sit together if they're a family,
          or if not, at least to share a few moments together.
They would also be asked to break open the readings of the Sunday
     using the Question of the Week
     and the faith sharing process within the parish.

Guide to More Meaningful Classrooms

Connected to the whole community

There are many reasons for a parish or school
    to continue using traditional classrooms or meeting spaces
    and the "schoolhouse framework"
        to provide instruction and education in the faith.
It's what people have come to expect at the parish.
    It is always difficult to change expectations
    and sometimes can cause painful divisions.
For some parishes and for some entire dioceses,
    retaining use of the classroom will seem best.
But beyond that,
    the classroom is an effective way to provide instruction
        and do formal teaching associated with catechesis.
There are times when children will learn better,
    as adults will,
    by being in age-similar groups in classrooms.
If that is the case in your parish,
    there are some powerful ways you can implement
    whole community catechesis,
    using the classroom as a springboard for the process.

First, make it a practice in your parish to recruit needed catechists
    by first providing some discernment
    to help folks know whether they have the gift of teaching.
As we said earlier, teaching is a gift of the Holy Spirit
    that not everyone receives.
Those who do have this gift are called to share it
    with the whole community.

Second, make wide use of faith sharing
    to provide opportunities for conversion.
        Begin every session
        with some form of faith sharing that leads
            to deeper reflection on the mysteries under study.

Third, if at all possible, connect that faith sharing
    to the Sunday assembly and Liturgy of the Word
    by breaking open the Word proclaimed there
        in the way described in this handbook.
This is not a mere suggestion.

The Sunday liturgy is the "source and summit" of the Christian life,
    as we have noted earlier.
Many people who come to our schools or faith formation programs,
    often do not show up on Sundays.
By breaking open the Word after the assembly
    and using that as the basis for sharing faith,
    everything is connected.

Fourth, employ a spiral scope and sequence
    that allows you to extend what is happening
        in your program
        to the whole community.
There are suggestions on how to do this in chapter four.

And fifth, do not fail to teach extensively
    on the rich treasure
    that is Catholic social teaching.
The gospel is not a work of literature
    to read and appreciate and file for later.
It contains the teachings of Jesus—all of them!
And reflection on that gospel in light of those teachings
    leads us without fail to become
        peacemakers,
        justice seekers,
        workers in the vineyard,
            willing to feed the hungry,
            give drink to the thirsty,
            clothing to the naked,
            to befriend the imprisoned,
            and to set free all those now held in bondage.
Catholic social teaching is the body of teachings
    that helps us see what the gospel demands of us.
By bringing this teaching into faith formation in positive ways
    as a vital part of the curriculum,
    you help the learners come to know
        how to *live their faith*.

These five steps are a wonderful way
    to connect religion sessions to the whole community of faith.

Plan for Catechesis Assemblies

Bring the whole community together

The traditional class session, we have said,
    is a good way for some parishes
    to provide catechesis to their whole community.
But for others, the meeting space is being expanded,
    or several groups of learners are being combined,
        to form a larger assembly.
These larger assemblies are often intergenerational,
    they often include liturgical prayer,
    and they assume many formats.
An assembly typically combines many smaller groups
    into a single, large group
    led by a master or lead catechist
        who has the gift of teaching,
        has the vocation of catechist,
        and is paid a stipend for his or her work.

The term assembly
    emerges from the Sunday assembly.
We Christians assemble with one another
    for many purposes:
        for Eucharist,
        to break open the Word,
        to fight for justice in the world,
        to share our journeys of faith,
        and now to engage in catechesis.
Within the assembly hall,
    which is what we name it,
    are many round tables,
        a podium,
        a projection screen if needed,
        a table for food,
        and perhaps other things.
At each round table sit five to eight learners,
    plus their table leaders.
The table leaders will mainly come from the ranks
    of those who are catechists in religion sessions.
The primary task of preparation
    for each assembly
    falls on the parish staff and lead catechists.

Table leaders provide supervision and organization.
Sometimes age groups will be combined
    to form a single assembly.
Other times, an assembly will be composed
    of a single age group only,
    along with the leaders.
For example,
    depending on the size of the program,
    the entire second and third grades may meet together—
        all in one large room,
        along with parents or sponsors
        grandparents,
        interested parishioners,
        and some of the staff—
    all for the purpose of sharing catechesis
    and learning more about the faith.
The first year they may follow the second grade textbook,
    and the following year the third grade book.

If the parish is large enough,
    perhaps just the third grade meets in one room.
If the parish is small,
    all three grades may meet at one time.
On the other hand, the assembly might be composed
    mainly of adults:
    for example, those in liturgical ministries
    meeting together in a series of catechesis assemblies,
        along with other parish leaders
        who are preparing for liturgical roles
        or who want to know more about liturgy.
In this group you might also have older youngsters
    who are not yet confirmed,
    neophytes in their first years of Christian life,
        or others.

A typical assembly

Here's what happens
    on a typical evening.
The learners sit at round tables
    accompanied by as many of their parents/sponsors as possible.
The parents, grandparents, godparents,
    or other interested parishioners
    serve as sponsors for the younger learners.

Parents readily come forward as table leaders or sponsors
    but so do others in the parish,
    many of them former classroom catechists
    whom we used to recruit the hard way!

Within two or three weeks of the beginning of this new approach,
    word will get out within the parish
    that it is much easier to be a table leader
        than it had been to be a catechist in a classroom.
Parents will begin attending every week.
    They will be encouraged to do so by the program,
    and they'll be there because it isn't as threatening
        as showing up in the back of a religion session.
When a parent shows up to visit a classroom
    in a school or a faith formation program
    everyone's uncomfortable:
        the parents, their child,
        and the teacher or catechist.
In this new approach that discomfort is eliminated
    because the assemblies are *designed*
    to have parents present.
If parents still choose not to participate,
    their children will come under the care of others
        at the table.
Thus any given table will have five to eight learners,
    accompanied by several adults.

Retain the use of your religion textbook series,
    but instead of marching through it front-to-back,
    use it as a resource.
The lead catechists
    and parish director of whole community catechesis
    plan each assembly very carefully,
        balancing liturgy,
        quiet time,
        sharing at the tables,
        and instruction right out of the book.
We all love our parish volunteer catechists!
    Boy do they have heart!
However, they themselves often feel they are not fully prepared
    for their roles.
They work so hard to keep order
    and do an adequate job
    in those religion sessions.

When you ask them about it,
    they'll tell you that they feel relieved
    not to be responsible on their own
        for the faith of the learners.
As table leaders,
    their role in preparing and leading the session
        is greatly reduced.

The assemblies are guided by a lead catechist
    who is paid a small stipend,
    has the gift of teaching,
    and is very well prepared each week.
These lead catechists are drawn
    from the ranks of the volunteers;
    they are persons who feel a genuine vocation to teach.
This person leads the catechetical process
    for the entire room,
    using a microphone.
I can't emphasize enough how important
    the gift of teaching is to this process.
It is one of the biggest changes you will experience.
More and more catechetical leaders are realizing
    that many of our well-meaning volunteers
    do not have that gift.
They have big hearts,
    free time,
    and kids in the program themselves,
        but sometimes not the gift of teaching.
However, as gifted teachers are discovered in your parish,
    the Spirit will be unleashed here!
Such teachers can really "hold a crowd"
    and help them learn!

Here's how this works during a typical assembly.
The lead catechist calls the evening to order.
    He or she introduces any guests in the room
    and makes sure everyone is situated.
If the pastor or other priests
    or parish staff members are present,
    the catechist introduces them as well.
Don't forget the musicians!

Then the lead catechist turns to the musicians
    to lead a peppy opening song.

From that song, the lead catechist
  moves directly to the Question of the Week
  and faith sharing.
The gospel is proclaimed as on Sunday,
  the responsorial psalm may be sung again,
  then the sharing is led by the table leaders.
To end the faith sharing,
  sing a verse of that song again!

After that
  the lead catechist introduces the evening topic,
  which is usually based on a lesson from the religion text.
Following that introduction
  everyone turns back to the tables for a little more sharing,
  or perhaps some other activity to help them focus.
The lead catechist might then ask for everyone's attention
  and move to a video clip related to the evening's topic,
  using volunteers skilled in technology.
Those technology volunteers are becoming vital!
They'll also help make sure the PowerPoint is running smoothly,
  or the overhead projector is ready (with working bulbs!),
  or the slide projector is set to go,
  or the music is ready to play,
  or the lights can be dimmed when needed,
  or the microphone is working,
    and so forth.

Using the catechist's edition of the religion text,
  the lead catechist will prompt the movement
  to a deeper look at some doctrine and content.
Here the table leaders play a vital role,
  but have little if any preparation to do beforehand.
This content period may last twenty or thirty minutes
  and may include some reading at the tables,
  some sharing,
  some activities,
  and some response on the part of the learners.
When it's appropriate again,
  the movement shifts back to the lead catechist,
  maybe for a quick presentation,
    outlining essentials of the faith,
    referring to the textbook
    to emphasize key points.

Then back to the tables for an activity,
    to help shore up the learning.
By then it's time for a break
    and food is always included in that!
Based on what we read in the gospels,
    you really can't expect a post-resurrection
    appearance of the risen Lord
        without sharing food first.

After the break,
    refocus everyone with a little more singing,
        maybe even a prayer service
        from the textbook,
    and then another activity to focus
    before moving on for more learning,
        connections to liturgy,
        to Scripture,
        to daily life.
Finally, plan an activity to help the household
    live according to what was just learned.
With so many of the parents present
    you have a real chance of sending this home!

Surprise folks by changing the format.
    Each assembly should gather biweekly
    because people get to know one another better,
    but vary the format session to session.
    Use all the options available.
Cover the main points in the text.
    The bishops of the Church rightly expect us
    to provide everyone with a comprehensive treatment
        of the fundamentals of our faith.

These assemblies are an answer to prayer!
They mix excellent catechesis
    with fine group liturgical prayer and music.
They use well-prepared media
    mixed with quiet times of prayer
    with the lights turned low.
These assemblies welcome parents in ways that classrooms cannot
    and they welcome the rest of the community, too.
Such assemblies provide solid catechesis with excellent pedagogy,
    and it's for the *whole community*!

In addition, those table leaders will really enjoy their ministry!
By the fourth week
> you'll have many more leaders than you need,
>
> but it won't matter
>
> because in a catechesis assembly,
>> there's room for everyone
>>
>> and everyone learns from each other!

Finding leaders for each table
> is actually the easy part.

For one thing, table leaders
> do not have to commit themselves
>
> to elaborate lesson planning or preparation.

For another, they know
> they will not face the challenges
>> of teaching children or teens in a group.

Beyond all that,
> they themselves will grow in their faith.

Here is the miracle of these assemblies.
> Suddenly catechesis and religious education become
>> an exciting biweekly event in the parish
>>
>> to which everyone is invited
>>
>> and to which most people look forward.

This form of catechesis slowly becomes what its name says:
> *whole* community catechesis.

In addition, recruiting volunteers
> for the different age groups is no longer needed,
>> to everyone's delight!

And besides that,
> as parishes make this shift,
>
> their test scores go up!

Learners learn more in this setting.

Other staff who contribute to the assemblies:
> 1. someone to coordinate hospitality (food and beverages);
> 2. someone to run electronic equipment;
> 3. one or two ushers to help welcome folks,
>> distribute or collect items,
>>
>> or perform other service duties;
> 4. folks to help with prayer and music;
> 5. folks to help take down and clean up.

Planning

The assemblies are planned by the lead catechists,
    working with the parish director,
    parish liturgical musicians,
        and others.
You might even consider forming a small team
    within the parish for this purpose.
In some parishes, the pastor will join in the planning.
Planning and even a little rehearsal
    with the technology volunteer
    or musicians
    or others
        is essential.
Consider running your assembly
    for about a two-hour period.
That's not much longer than most feature films
    or television shows.
It's long enough to require a food break,
    which is good for socializing,
    an element missing from most faith formation programs.
Even for younger children,
    the current fifty-minute period
    used in most parishes
        simply isn't long enough
        to accomplish much.

In terms of the space needed,
    the parish basement or meeting hall, if you have one,
    works very well.
The dining room or the gym in the school
    are also possibilities.
For the youngest children,
    consider using a large piece of carpet
    rolled out on the floor of one of these rooms.
If you don't own round tables,
    ask one of the societies in the parish
    (for example, the Knights of Columbus
        or the Catholic Daughters)
    to help you pay for them.
If you don't have a large enough room,
    look for one in the neighborhood,
    at another church,
    at a local fraternal hall,
    or in the public schools.

The food

Now here's a wonderful new ministry
    for all those great epicures in the parish,
    or for anyone else who likes to cook.
It is a longstanding custom for Christians
    to gather with their gifts of food,
    to bring them together,
        and to share them.
At these assemblies,
    part of the festive spirit
    and sense of forming the Church
        that emerges
        comes from sharing food together.

Summertime

We currently plan our catechetical year
    around the public school year calendar.
This means we shut down our programs during most
    of the feasts and holy days
    that are important to us as Christians.
We're never around during Christmas,
    reducing Advent to early Christmas.
    We're gone during Holy Week;
    if Pentecost falls anytime after mid-May,
        we're gone then, too.
Pentecost may well be one of the most significant
    moments of catechesis
    in the entire year, yet we seldom observe it.
Instead, if we run assemblies or classroom sessions every other week,
    twelve months per year,
    we will hold assemblies in the summer.
However, summer assemblies or classes can be more laid back,
    with a more casual and intimate
    atmosphere and spirit.
They can be a time for reflection,
    with long evenings
    and parish picnics and outings.
For example, a Saturday afternoon assembly-picnic
    might culminate in a huge outdoor
    eucharistic assembly.

Getting started

Catechesis assemblies
    don't begin from nothing.
The springboard for the whole community
    is the present children's program.
You already have some level
    of children's catechesis
    going on in your parish.
Use that as the entry point
    to these catechesis assemblies or more meaningful classroom sessions,
    and involve the rest of the parish community at the same time.

Use the people,
    large spaces,
    schedules,
    and resources
        now at the disposal of children's programming
        to establish this whole community approach.
Start slowly.
    If going into this "cold turkey"
    won't work at your parish,
        then don't try it!
Organize assemblies for one or two grade levels,
    or hold one assembly per month for a while,
    or take the time to plan for this, if needed.
The thing not to do
    is to ignore the features and principles
    of whole community catechesis.
People of the next generation expect an approach
    that suits them,
    that involves them in the process.

In the spirit of Vatican II
    we must listen to the signs of the times,
    root ourselves in the long tradition of the Church,
    and then reform and update ourselves
        to meet the current demands.
The principal virtues needed here,
    as Pope John XXIII said so well,
    are courage and hope.
We have reason to be optimistic
    in the light of the Spirit.

The role of the pastor and staff

We would never consider
    holding a Sunday assembly
    without having the pastor present.
For us Catholics, our pastors are key
    to our community life.
They are the ones whose job it is
    to bring "holy order" to the parish,
    taking a sort of executive role.
This is no accident.
Having such "order bringers" among us
    is a gift of the Holy Spirit.
It's how the Church is led and organized.
So having the pastor or pastoral associate
    present for these assemblies,
    even if only for part of them,
        is very important, even essential.
In our current framework, of course,
    with multiple classrooms
    all meeting simultaneously,
        such pastoral presence is impossible.
But in catechesis assemblies
    it's very possible,
    and the planners should carve out a role
        for the pastor or pastoral associate.
The same is true for the pastoral staff.
    When it's possible for them to be present,
    they should be introduced and enabled to participate.
This is how learners come to understand
    the local Church:
    by meeting its leaders firsthand.

Borrowing from the catechumenate

Whether you're using classroom sessions or assemblies,
    whole community catechesis borrows heavily
        from the catechumenate,
        an ancient and wise method of helping folks
            learn what it means to follow Christ.
First, of course, is a form of "mystagogy."
    In this case it's a reflection
    on the mysteries of daily life
        by means of the Question of the Week.

Second, the assemblies employ table leaders.
Even if you choose not to have a sponsor for each learner,
    the table leaders act almost like sponsors do
        in the catechumenate.
And in classroom sessions, too, learners can be given a sponsor.
We would never think of proceeding
    in the catechumenate
    unless each candidate or catechumen
        had a proper sponsor.
This is true in whole community catechesis.
    The table leaders play a vital role
    in the life of the disciples.
They are role models,
    witnesses,
    and facilitators.

Third, whole community catechesis relies heavily
    on the teaching power of the rites of the Church.
In the assemblies,
    it's possible to introduce whole elements
    from the Church's rites.
In the classroom sessions, care must be taken to include these rites as well,
    either by means of video or other media presentations,
    or under the leadership of the catechists.
Here we pray the rites and let them teach.

We might even consider whole community catechesis
    to be *inspired* by the catechumenate,
    which is in accord with the wishes
    of the *General Directory for Catechesis*.
Beyond that, everything done
    in whole community catechesis
    has its source and summit
        in the Sunday assembly.
There, the introduction of newcomers
    is traditionally made,
    just as in the catechesis assemblies.
The members of parish households
    come from their own dining room tables
    to share a common meal.
        Here, too, households join the assembly
        as a whole and bring their lives with them.

In the catechumenate, the Word is broken open in the homily,
    just as in the faith sharing
    which begins each assembly or class session.
The body of Christ is shared
    while here the body of Christ is assembled
        to grow and celebrate its faith.
From the assembly,
    the catechumens go forth to live their faith in everyday life,
    just as learners leave the catechesis assembly or classroom session
        to shape the place where they live
        as a "household of faith."

Choose the approach that works for you

If you think that you might want to
    create more meaningful religion sessions
    but also plan for catechesis assemblies,
        why not try a combination of the two?
This approach is right for many parishes today.
    It allows you to retain the smaller group sessions
    but to add a catechesis assembly
    once each month or so
        to provide a forum
        for parents and other parishioners
        to become involved directly in the process.
This combination approach,
    using classrooms plus occasional assemblies,
    is a great way to shift gears slowly
        and gradually bring parents into the process.
You could hold regular sessions two nights each month,
    or daily in the school,
    and then plan for a monthly assembly besides.

For some parishes,
    the right approach might be
        to stop using the classroom sessions altogether.
For most of these parishes, holding an assembly
    every other week is the best schedule.
For one thing, catechesis assemblies
    are a couple of hours long
    rather than a mere fifty minutes.
Furthermore, many parishes hold these assemblies
    every other week *all year round.*
    (The summer assemblies are some of the best!)

Having twenty-six assemblies per year
    allows parishes to cover every chapter
        in the religion text
    and to celebrate the liturgical year
    without skipping any major feasts or seasons.
For other parishes, the best choice is to shift to catechesis assemblies
    but conduct religion sessions only
    during the regular children's school year.
For schools,
    the most workable solution
    is to conduct religion sessions as usual,
    but add an assembly every other week
        at the end of the day on Thursday.
Invite parents to come home early from work
    or to attend if they're already home.
Invite grandparents,
    senior members of the parish,
    and anyone else who's interested in formation
        to participate.

Within the framework of the catechesis assembly,
    there are also two options.
One is to hold the assemblies on an intergenerational basis,
    inviting anyone who wishes to participate
    into the process.
Under this option, all participants of any age
    work together in the same room
    just as we worship together in the Sunday assembly.

A second is to begin the assemblies with all present,
    but then to separate the adults from the youth
    and hold age-specific sessions.
Many believe that there is good reason
    to allow folks of the same age
    to explore and learn together.

Within these options,
    each parish can find a way
    to incorporate the principles
        of whole community catechesis
        into its catechetical process.
No parish need continue to provide
    faith formation for children only,
    without addressing the whole community.

CHAPTER SIX

Developing Households of Faith

The centrality of supper

Nothing is more important to the success
    of whole community catechesis
    than that we who live in the households of the parish
        plan,
        prepare for,
        cook together,
        sit down to eat,
        linger as long as possible at,
        clean up together,
        and savor
            the evening meal.
Nothing is more important.

Supper is the memorial meal
    left to us by Christ himself.
That great meal is, of course,
    the supper on which today's liturgy
    in the Sunday assembly
        is built.
But the immediate preparation for that assembly
    is supper.
Anyone who is eating supper with others
    on a regular basis,
    even if it's once or twice a month,
        will tell you how important it is.
Anyone who is in love with another
    will list the memories of great times
    as a record of meals and celebrations
        at table.
Anyone whose family regularly
    shares supper,
    or Sunday breakfast after Mass,
    or early coffee before the day begins,
        can tell you how important this is.
Anyone who has lost a spouse to death,
    or sometimes even to divorce,
    will tell you that they miss those meals,
        the shopping they did for them,
        the cooking,
        even the cleanup afterward.

Anyone who has close friends
    looks forward and even longs
    for those times when meals are shared!
Even in homes where love has gone cold,
    where there is a violent or dark temper
        dominating the household—
        even there, meals are important.
Sometimes those meals explode in rage
    and sometimes they are times of peace,
    but they remain important.

A great friend of mine once told me
    that she never needed counseling
    to bring her together with her kids
        because they washed dishes together
        every evening.
Of course, in the washing and sweeping up
    there were fights sometimes,
    but there were also natural moments
        of tremendous intimacy.
Things work out when you cook and wash dishes
    together.
It's hard to sit down to table
    with someone you haven't forgiven.

Organize the parish around meals

So what would happen if we organized our parishes
    around making suppertime sacred,
    rather than organizing parish meetings
        during the supper hour?
I once knew a bishop who traveled to parishes,
    helping provide adult education
    within the diocese he served.
        I often traveled with him.
We'd leave the pastoral center about 3:00 PM,
    usually heading west into the sunset,
    due to arrive at our destination by 5:30,
        in time for supper.
This bishop would urge the people
    to make time to share meals.
He knew that if they shared meals,
    they would share on a deeper level, too.

He knew they would experience the risen Lord
    in the context of those meals,
    just as the early disciples did:
        the fish fry on the beach in John's gospel,
        at Emmaus during supper,
        in the upper room: let's eat!
He knew that shared meals,
    mostly in homes
    but sometimes also at the parish level,
        are naturally catechetical.
As people share the stories of their respective days,
    a common thread emerges.
    People catechize each other
        with insights,
        with compassion,
        with charity and mercy and forgiveness.
This natural catechesis leads inevitably
    to a *desire* for more formal instruction.
Such a desire, which arises from the shared moments of life,
    is the key
    without which no adult faith formation can occur.

In the earliest Christian communities the meal was the occasion
    in which Christ's presence
    was more fully recognized,
        more fully real.
We need this.
    We're human, after all.
We need the signs and symbols
    and sacraments of our faith
    to heal and guide and, yes,
        sometimes to cajole us.

In whole community catechesis,
    shared meals are really the basis
    for the evangelization, catechesis,
    and instruction in the faith
    of the whole community.
Whatever materials we develop for this purpose,
    should be useful at table
        somehow.
Not that the suppers we share have to be eaten
    with a guidebook in hand.

The only guide we need is a good cookbook.
    However, sometimes we can push back the dishes
        and consider our faith more formally.
At these times we might need a short faith instruction,
    to give us something to think about
    and integrate into our lives.

The households of our lives

Now, it's safe to say that
    each of us lives in a household of some kind.
The household—the people and pets and plants—
    together make daily life possible.
The household might live in an apartment,
    a house,
    a condo,
    a mobile home,
    or even a single room,
        but to the members it's home.
The household is the place where we
    live our everyday lives.
It's where we keep our things,
    where we get our mail,
    and where we welcome guests.
Even when we're away from our homes,
    on vacation,
    running errands,
    or working at a job,
        home is still home.
The people who make up your household
    might include a spouse,
    or partner,
    or kids,
    or a roommate,
    or parents.
People who live together usually make decisions
    and plan their lives
    taking the others into account.
When we use the term "family"
    to define those with whom we live,
    we usually mean people related to us
        by blood lines,
    or people we're married to,
    or our own kids.

But a family can also be "blended,"
    meaning that more than one blood line
    is living in that home
    because of a second or third marriage.
        Sometimes without that second marriage,
        the parents have just taken up living together.
All this coming and going in marriage
    can be very confusing.
A single household might easily have people living in it
    with three or four different last names.
These multiple blood lines taking up home life together
    are often called blended families.

In many households,
    of course,
    the people aren't married at all.
In some cases, it's because marriage is not allowed,
    as in gay or lesbian partnerships,
    where they are bonded for life
    and living in a marriage-like relationship,
        but not legally married
        or even sanctioned by the Church.
In other cases, the couple is straight,
    but they've had a bad experience
    with marriage
        and have decided to forego it.
In certain cases, those living in the household
    just aren't sure where their place is in life
        or in love.
    They're barely able to get from day to day
        holding it together,
        much less enter a marriage.
In still other cases,
    there is just plain sexual satisfaction involved.
        The couple doesn't want commitment.

A lot of us also live alone,
    more than at any previous time in history.
When you walk through a grocery store these days
    it's easy to see that many items are packaged
    for people who eat alone.
Many new homes don't even have dining rooms
    in them anymore.

The expectation that a family of some kind
	will sit down to a cooked meal at a table
	and linger there over supper is very low.
In fact, if you did a survey,
	probably many people would tell you
	that when they eat alone,
		they do it standing up at their kitchen sink
		or sitting down in front of the TV.
When you eat alone,
	it's hard to set a table
	and light a candle
	and make it romantic.
The whole idea behind romance,
	after all,
	is to be with someone else whom you love.
However, folks who live alone do still maintain
	a household.
This household might be made up of people
	living in several different physical places,
	but they gather like a family,
	sharing occasional meals,
	giving each other support,
	and celebrating life's occasions.

All across the United States,
	people are also living without a home.
We often call these folks the homeless,
	and for us they rarely have a real face.
They disappear in society,
	under the bridge,
	or behind the warehouse,
	or right in front of us as we walk down the sidewalk,
		sleeping on a grate for heat.
But they all have a memory
	or a dream
		of home.

These people without homes,
	however,
	often do maintain a loose sort of household
		with others in their circles.
They support each other,
	know each other,
	and share what little they have with each other.

In fact, it's possible that folks sharing
    the loose households of homelessness
    have more happiness,
        and more love,
        than the wealthiest intact family
        living in a big old house
        with their every need or want supplied.

Even the aged members of our cultures—
    when they live in nursing homes
    homes for the elderly, retirement homes, and so on—
        do still live within a household.
Their household might be that of a child
    living nearby,
    with whose family they gather often.
On the other hand, they may rarely see their children
    any longer,
    and now their household is very small:
        that visitor from church
        and roommates in the home.

Only a very few people actually live
    with no reference to anyone else whatsoever,
    with no household at all.

The church of the home

When we Christians say we belong to a Church,
    we don't usually mean
    that we belong to a physical building
    with the cross on top.
The building with the cross on top
    is only the assembly hall and offices
        of the church, where we meet.
When we say we belong to a Church,
    we also don't usually mean
    that we belong to the pope and bishops.
Actually, they sort of belong to us as Church members.

Down through the years there's been a misunderstanding
    about what it means to belong to a Church.
We had come to believe that what was sacred
    happened only at the building
    with the cross on top,

which, increasingly,
we also called the church.
By sacred we were referring to things like
getting blessed,
or praying together,
or learning about religion,
or having really holy things
like tabernacles,
and incense,
and holy water,
and altars.
All those things were found only
at the building with the cross on top.
The people who resided or worked
at that building with the cross on top
were holy, too.
They wore special clothes
and never married
and were the ones who performed
all the holy rites and ceremonies.

We took this very seriously.
We would not even consider
using a holy card
or a new rosary
if it had not first been blessed by a priest.
We lived in the world,
and on Sundays we went to church.
That's the language we used to describe it.

Recently we've also added a few lay people
to the people in the Church
who are part of what's sacred.
They're the parish staff people,
and certain key leaders.
They recruit the rest of us as "volunteers"
at the parish church
to work as ministers there.
They solicit our money
as donations to the Church.
They help us understand what the Church teaches,
and they provide for
those moments of prayer and celebration
which are part of the Church:

baptism,

marriage,

funerals,

illness,

Sunday Mass,

and others.

In all of this, we mainly understand

    that "they" are the Church

    and we participate in it

        because the rest of us don't live or work

        at the parish church.

We attend Mass

    or volunteer

    or give our money there,

        but we *live* in the world.

I'm not sure anyone really believes this any more,

    but there was a time not so long ago

    when most people saw the Church as holy

        and the world as not holy.

In fact, most of the time the world was seen as downright sinful.

It's full of people making money,

    having sex,

    drinking liquor,

    watching ball games,

    and so forth.

Each of these activities was seen as somewhat unholy

    compared to what we did at church.

Each was, in fact,

    a "proximate occasion of sin"

    if we weren't careful.

We go to church,

    we would say,

    to confess our sins

    and be returned to a holy state.

Then we went out and plunged right back

    into that nasty old secular world.

The secular and the sacred were separated

    by a great divide.

The secular world was where we lived

    our everyday lives

    and the sacred world was "at church."

This way of thinking is called "dualism"
    because it sees dual worlds:
        one holy
        and the other profane.
It grew out of a philosophy
    which sees the world as composed
    of these two opposing forces.

The holy fights against the unholy.
The worldly is in contradiction to
    and competition with
    the holy for our hearts and minds.
One cannot balance them.
    Either a person is holy or not.

However, in recent years
    much of this way of thinking has been corrected,
    and the correction is this:
    there is no divide between the sacred and the secular.
We *are* the Church.
Our homes are where the Church lives
    every single day.
The parish buildings are where we assemble
    and carry on some of our business,
    but most of the business of the Church
    happens right here in our homes.
        We live in the Church.

Of course, when I say that we live in the Church,
    I don't mean
    that we live at the parish.
I mean that our homes—
    whatever configuration of people live there,
    and whatever kind of housing we live in—
    our homes are where the Church lives.
This is why homemaking
    is so important to Christians
    and all religious people—
because when we make home, we also make Church.
Indeed,
    we do still have and need our parishes.
    We need those buildings with a cross on top.

The parish is a sort of resource center
    and gathering place
    and sign of God's love
    and mystery imbued with God's presence.
It provides us with what we need to live as Church, that is,
    to live well in our homes.
So it becomes a two-way street.
We join a parish and provide it with resources
    (money, time, presence)
    and it provides us with resources in return
    (the Sunday assembly, training, pastoral care).
        It's a fifty-fifty deal.

Here's the rub:
    once the Church moves out of its parish buildings
    and into the homes of the people,
        everything changes.
At home the Church is naturally inclusive.
In many homes, for example,
    women preside at table on a regular basis.
Reconciliation is either free flowing or not
    but is woven into everyday life.
Here we celebrate real meals;
    we struggle with financial worries
    over morning coffee.
Here we seek love in our lives,
    peace,
    happiness,
    or a little rest.
People might argue that so much of what happens
    at home is not holy:
    all those blended families,
        unmarried parents,
        and others who are not living "right."
Yet in the real world of everyday life,
    this is how people seek love.
It might not be the perfect model which theologians seek,
    but it's how real people live.
This is precisely where catechesis
    must be most effective
because the household is where what's taught
    in catechesis
    is lived.
We cannot pretend anything else is real.

In these households,
 there's a lot of interference.
The television is on.
 We're logged on to the Internet.
 There's a stack of half-read magazines
  in the bathroom.

We have two or three jobs
 or none at all at the moment.
The kids have busy schedules,
 mom needs more care as she ages,
 we agreed to work on the neighborhood clean-up campaign,
 and there's a pile of recycling waiting at the door.
 Suddenly the phone rings,
  and it's the parish calling
  for volunteers
  to teach religious education classes
  on Wednesday nights until May.
   Gasp!

Above all, love happens at home.
Oh yes, we do love our fellow parishioners,
 but that's a remote,
 general kind of love.
We may have close friends
 in the congregation,
 or other family members whom we love,
 but that love is not a result
  of being in the same parish.
The love we have at home is intimate,
 romantic,
 personal,
 and lived in everyday life.
  And sometimes love is cold,
   distant,
   silent,
   or lost.

When the gospel speaks of love,
 it isn't describing a remote form
 of regard for each other.
"Love one another as I have loved you" (Jn 13:34)

Five suggestions

As you begin to develop
    an approach to catechesis that embraces
    the whole community,
        don't be tempted to skip this dimension.
The development of households of faith
    is part and parcel of the work of the Church,
    not a sideline to everything else.
Here are some ways to get started immediately.

First and most important,
    teach about Christian homemaking.
Help folks learn how to set a table for a shared supper,
    how to plan a meal,
    how to celebrate feast days, birthdays, different anniversaries
        in a Christian way,
    how to entertain guests in their homes,
    how to make any meal more special
        (even at a fast food restaurant),
    how to share different forms of entertainment,
    how to make the house more welcoming,
    how to add romance to everyday life.
Cooking and decorating classes,
    even if they teach how to make a simple soup supper
    or fix a centerpiece,
    might send a clear message.
Toward this end, the parish might have to hold
    its evening meetings at a time
    other than the supper hour.

Second, offer to send home instruction in the faith,
    based on the whole community scope and sequence
    described above.
        Some will want this and some won't.
        Just keep offering,
            keep putting Church teachings into plain English,
            keep offering the resources.
Using a spiral scope and sequence,
    tailor all your parish programs to deal with the same theme
    so that everyone in the parish is on the same page:
        parents are learning what their children are,
        Sunday liturgies lead to faith sharing,
        and the whole community grows in faith.

Third, if you offer the Living with Christ retreats,
    provide a follow up resource
    to help participants carry the message home with them.

Fourth, create a series of "household kits"
    that have in them items with which a typical household
    can be reminded to live their faith.
        Items might include:
            ■ holy water and a card about its significance,

            ■ a special candle,

            ■ a table top conversation starter with provocative questions,

            ■ a book of prayers for the domestic Church,

            ■ family blessings, but only one or two at a time

            ■ a monthly guide to the saints.

Fifth, send home the faith sharing Question of the Week
    and help folks see the importance
    of sharing at home.
        Some will and some won't.
        Don't criticize or nag but keep offering.

CHAPTER SEVEN

Bulletin Short Courses

Using your bulletin effectively for
Whole Community Catechesis

Introduction

A bulletin short course
 is a series of very short articles which,
 taken together,
 provide a full explanation
  of the various elements
  of whole community catechesis.
The courses are presented in question and answer format,
 but you should feel free to ask and answer questions
 that your particular community might have
 which aren't included here.
You have permission to reprint these
 in any way you wish.
Some parishes print them week after week
 in the bulletin, in a special section
  devoted to preparing the whole community
   to understand the real meaning of catechesis
   and its place in each member's life.
Other parishes gather
 articles on a single topic
 and publish them as a flier.
Some parishes post these on their web sites,
and others use them at parish meetings,
 one per meeting,
 allowing time for discussion of the elements
  so the leaders develop a deeper understanding.

Catholic parish leaders can sometimes
      become preoccupied with church structures:
            buildings,
            heating and cooling systems,
            parking lots,
            employee benefits,
            budgets,
            and other structural details.
However, whole community catechesis
      calls all parish leaders
      to first be men and women
            who know Christ
            and who live their faith every day.
The first and most critical task of the parish
      is to help folks meet Christ,
      and nothing can replace that.

The Church serves as a sign of God's presence,
      a mystery here in our midst,
      a people gathered in the Spirit,
      a community and its leaders,
      an assembly of Jesus' followers,
            gathered to proclaim the Word,
            to break the bread,
            and to love each other.
If we spend all our time worrying about our buildings,
      we might overlook this more central task.
The Church is holy,
      not because it's perfect,
      or because the budget balances,
      or because the leaders say so,
            but because God's grace is present here.
Our task is to make sure the Church serves
      its most real, most holy purpose
      by making sure that we as leaders
            are living in Christ ourselves.

Q. WHAT EXACTLY IS WHOLE COMMUNITY CATECHESIS?

A. Whole community catechesis
is an approach to parish or school religious education
through which youth and adults as well as children
are invited to participate
in faith formation programs throughout the year.
The entire community thus becomes the focus of all we do in catechesis.

In whole community catechesis,
what happens in the Sunday assembly for Mass
is closely connected to what happens
in the religious education classroom.
The liturgy of the Word from Sunday is the starting point.
Catechesis or faith formation
must flow from that Word
and each learner is invited to "break open the Word,"
to share their faith about what they believe.

Also in whole community catechesis,
parents play a vital role
alongside all the other members of the community.
Catechesis is not just for children!
It's for everyone.
Every Catholic is invited to know and love the Church,
to walk with Christ in his or her daily life,
and to gather faithfully together on Sunday for the parish Mass.

Added to that, whole community catechesis
places great emphasis on developing households of faith.
It's certainly true for a child,
but also true for everyone,
that no matter how effective
our experience of faith might be at the parish level,
what really counts is how we live that faith
in our everyday lives at home!
If our homes are not places where the faith is shared and lived,
then the work of catechesis is like sowing seed on rocky ground.

Q. WHY ARE WE CHANGING THE LANGUAGE?

Why can't we continue calling it
>CCD
>or religious ed
>or religion class?

A. At Vatican II it was important
>for the bishops of the world,
>along with the pope,
>to refer to the Church using new language.

In order for the reform
>envisioned by Pope John XXIII
>to become reality,
>we needed a new way of speaking about the Church.

So, the bishops began to refer to the Church
>under a new name:
>>*the People of God.*

They knew that if the Church was called that,
>soon it would *become* that,
>>and they were right!

Likewise, the pope and bishops
>renewed our understanding of ourselves
>as part of the *Body of Christ.*

Refer to people as members of Christ's Body,
>they reasoned,
>and they will *become* Christ's Body
>>for the world.

The pope and bishops knew
>that language affects our perception of reality
>and, in turn, our actions:
>>if we call something by a new but true name
>>it becomes that thing!

The same is true for whole community catechesis.

How we name what we do is very important.
>*We will become what we call ourselves.*

If we continue calling our programs
>schools of religion,
>or religious education programs,
>or religion class,
>>most people will see them
>>as mainly for children.

However, if we call what we do by a new name,
>   *whole community catechesis,*
>   people will soon see it
>   as part and parcel of being Catholic.
We don't want to put new wine
>   into old wine skins, after all.
As Dick Reichert said in the
>   National Conference of Catechetical Leadership *Update* (No. 7):
"The real challenge contained
>   in the pursuit of alternative models
>   is to create a radical new paradigm
>   of catechesis.
It cannot simply be a process
>   of going back to the past
>   or making surface modifications
>   of the present models."
In other words, it isn't sufficient
>   to merely tinker with our present approach,
>   to shift the furniture in our present method
>   so the classrooms look different.
We can't merely invite the parents to participate.
As Dick Reichert noted,
>   we need a radical new paradigm
>   in order to achieve the goals
>   of the *General Directory for Catechesis.*

Q. WHAT NEW APPROACH TO RELIGIOUS EDUCATION DOES WHOLE COMMUNITY CATECHESIS OFFER?

A. Several features taken together
compose this new approach.

1. Conversion, the turning of our hearts to Christ,
   must become an essential part of every catechesis process.

2. The households must play an integral role
   in all that we do,
   and families must become more involved
   at the everyday level,
   not as occasional guests of the process.

3. The RCIA is our model;
   breaking open the Word is the approach
   that helps lead folks to ongoing conversion,
   love of Scripture,
   a heart for the materially poor,
   and deeper commitment to community life.

4. Adult education must become the norm,
   not the sideline.
   Catechesis is for adults
   as much as for children;
   in short,
   catechesis is the work of the whole community.

5. Catechists are called to a genuine vocation,
   not merely to fill the demand for personnel
   in our present programs.
   We need to discover the gift of teaching in others
   to allow the Spirit to work.

6. We must take care to teach precisely
   what the Church teaches,
   as outlined for us
   in the *Catechism of the Catholic Church.*
   Catechesis is not a time to teach our *opinions*
   about theology or life in the Church;
   it's the time to pass on faithfully
   what the Church hands on to us.

7. Finally, those who are in catechesis
   should see themselves as disciples of Christ
   on a lifelong journey of faith,
      not merely as temporary students
      completing a program that ends with graduation.

Whole community catechesis
   brings all these features
   into a single way of thinking,
      a single philosophy,
      a single focus for the parish.
It has the power to renew the whole community
   and to generate great enthusiasm
      for the gospel.

Q. IN WHOLE COMMUNITY CATECHESIS, DO WE STILL REFER TO THE PERSONS INVOLVED AS "STUDENTS"?

A. It would help tremendously
    to stop referring to people
    in our catechetical process
        as students.
In our culture the word "student"
    suggests academic learning,
    even if the meaning of the word
        could be broader.
It suggests a school year period of study,
    ending in graduation.
That ending is a key problem.
Nearly every adult in the Church today
    believes that he or she has completed
    their religious education.
        They're no longer students.
        They're adults now.
However, learning to follow the way of Christ
    never ends, as the bishops tell us in the GDC.
There is no graduation from catechesis;
    it's a lifelong journey of faith,
    a lifelong process.

So instead, why not give those engaged in faith formation
    another name?
Maybe we could call them simply "learners."
    A learner is one who is learning how
    to follow in the footsteps of Jesus,
        one who is learning a way of life.
This name suggests a never-ending, non-academic process
    of growing to live as Jesus taught us to.
Learner is a biblical word;
    anyone who refers to himself or herself as a learner
    is making a serious commitment to growth.
A learner is one who comes to encounter Christ
    not merely to know about him.
You may find the right term for your parish
    by asking those in catechesis
    what they would like to be called.
This change (no longer using the word "student")
    may be one of the most difficult to make
        at the parish level.

Why?
Because we have thought of those
   who are being formed in the faith
   as students for so long,
      in fact, for several generations.

The word is ingrained in the Catholic vocabulary
   of the present generation
   of parents and guardians.
On the other hand,
   all the efforts to change from student
      to learner
      or apprentice
   are worth it because
   the entire parish is thus re-educated
   about whole community catechesis.
When you announce that *anyone* who wishes
   to follow Christ more closely in his or her life
   may be part of the catechesis assemblies
      as a learning disciple,
      people will notice.
After all,
   we learned to refer to those in the catechumenate
   as catechumens or candidates,
      both words quite foreign to us at first.
We can make this change from student to learner as well
   if we put our hearts into it.

Q. WHERE DID THE IDEA FOR "WHOLE COMMUNITY CATECHESIS" COME FROM?

A. The whole movement toward an approach to catechesis
which involves the entire parish community
comes from four main sources.
First, catechetical leaders have given careful consideration
to the way Jesus taught,
as the *General Directory for Catechesis* suggests we should.
Second, we have all reflected seriously
on the teachings of Vatican II for more than forty years.
Third, the direction provided by the GDC itself
has been nothing other than revolutionary.
And fourth, there is an emerging consensus
in the catechetical community
that the present way we do our ministry,
in what's known as the "schoolhouse" framework,
just isn't working as well as we'd like it to.

Q. WHERE DID THE NAME "WHOLE COMMUNITY CATECHESIS" COME FROM?

A. The name, whole community catechesis,
comes directly from article #254 of the GDC, which says:
"The Christian community is the origin, locus,
and goal of catechesis.
Proclamation of the gospel always begins
with the Christian community and invites [people]
to conversion and the following of Christ.
It is the same whole community that welcomes
those who wish to know the Lord better
and permeate themselves with a new life.
The whole Christian community accompanies catechumens
and those being catechized,
and with maternal solicitude
makes them participate in her own experience
of the faith and incorporates them into herself."

Q. DO WE STILL HAVE RELIGIOUS INSTRUCTIONS?

A. Yes, indeed, there is a need for outright religious instruction
in order for Christian children to grow up and mature
in their faith.
Understanding the sacred Scriptures,
the Church's liturgy,
its history, devotions, and doctrines
is essential.
This is true for Christians of all age groups.
Our present schoolhouse framework does provide a structure
within which this outright religious education
happens very well.
The textbooks are complete and beautiful.
The students do seem to come away
with a pretty good working knowledge of the Church.

Q. BUT… WHAT'S MISSING?

A. Well, first of all, for us Catholics,
nothing can happen in the Church
that doesn't have its origin in the Sunday Mass.
For us, the liturgy is the "source and summit" of our faith.
It's what makes us truly Catholic.
So we must say that a real connection to the Sunday liturgy
is missing in most parishes.
How do we add that?
Whole community catechesis makes several suggestions:
• faith sharing based on the Sunday readings;
• some form of liturgical catechesis to help us understand the rites;
• use of a spiral scope and sequence in our textbook series.

Q. WHAT IS A "SPIRAL SCOPE AND SEQUENCE"?

A. First of all, a scope and sequence
is the organized framework,
the system of lessons and themes we follow
to present the teachings of the faith to a learner.
This framework follows a certain sequence of ideas,
one after the other.
It stays within a certain scope of topics and themes.
By providing this order for the presentation of the faith,
a learner has a better chance of getting it all right!
A spiral scope and sequence is one in which the learner
returns to each topic every year,
in spiral fashion.
Each time, the topics are presented in age-appropriate language
and teaching methods.
By using a spiral, all the students in a single parish or school (or both!)
can be studying the same theme at the same time,
making teacher preparation,
parent involvement,
intergenerational groupings,
and cross-cultural teaching much more possible!

Q. BEYOND THE SPIRAL SCOPE AND SEQUENCE, WHAT ELSE DOES WHOLE COMMUNITY CATECHESIS RECOMMEND?

A. In the past forty-five years
every single Church document
that deals with Christian education and catechesis
has insisted that parents and entire households
be involved in catechesis,
not just the children.
Without the rest of the household,
no matter how effective the religious education might be,
the child has little chance of developing deep faith roots
and living by Catholic customs and morality.
In whole community catechesis,
parishes plan for the involvement of the entire community,
based on the spiral scope and sequence mentioned earlier.
Not only are parents present
when their children are formed in the faith.
Much more radically,
households are being formed as Christian homes.

Q. HOW DO THE HOUSEHOLDS OF OUR PARISH GET INVOLVED IN WHOLE COMMUNITY CATECHESIS?

A. First, parishes invite every single household in the parish
    to take part in the faith sharing mentioned above,
    based on the readings from the Sunday assembly.
This faith sharing gives rise to the possibility
    of deeper and ongoing conversion to Christ.
The presence of Christ in the homes
    is the first step
    that will lead naturally to more prayer,
    to interpreting the events of the culture or world through Christian eyes,
    and to a desire for more catechesis.
Households might receive a kit of some kind,
    or suggestions about how to form a real home,
    sharing meals, and supporting one another as a family.

Q. IN OUR NEW WHOLE COMMUNITY APPROACH TO CATECHESIS, WHY IS THERE SO MUCH EMPHASIS ON CONVERSION?

A. For many Catholics growing up in the 1950s
    (and even for those who can't remember the 1950s),
    we thought conversion was for other Christians.
We even called them "converts"
    when they joined the Catholic Church.
Today we take a wider view,
    and we see that each Catholic
    also needs to turn his or her heart to Christ
        over and over again
        throughout their lives.
This turning is what we call conversion.
    The word comes from Latin,
    meaning literally, to turn.
The reason we emphasize it so much is that,
as the GDC teaches, conversion,
    the turning of one's heart to Christ,
    precedes catechesis.
Adults, like their kids,
    might sit through instructional classes,
    but until they turn their hearts to Christ
    and share that with others,
        we haven't really done our job
        of announcing the Good News of Christ.

INDEX OF REPRODUCIBLE HANDOUTS

Notes

Notes

Notes

Notes